My Child's Heart
Series 2

My Child's Heart
Series 2

Jesus
Our Savior and Friend

Kathy Kirk

Pleasant Word
A Division of WINEPRESS PUBLISHING

© 2008 by Kathy Kirk. All rights reserved.

© 2008 Photography: Lisa Landrum and Gino Santa-Maria

Pleasant Word (a division of WinePress Publishing, PO Box 428, Enumclaw, WA 98022) functions only as book publisher. As such, the ultimate design, content, editorial accuracy, and views expressed or implied in this work are those of the author.

No part of this publication may be reproduced, stored in a retrieval system, or transmitted in any way by any means—electronic, mechanical, photocopy, recording, or otherwise—without the prior permission of the copyright holder, except as provided by USA copyright law.

Content, Design, Photography and/or Cover may not be reproduced in whole or in part in any form without the express written consent of Kathy Kirk.

Unless otherwise designated, all Scriptures are from the *New American Standard Bible*® (NASB®) Copyright© The Lockman Foundation 1960, 1962, 1963, 1968, 1971, 1972, 1973, 1975, 1977, 1955. Used by permission.

Permission to quote from the following additional copyrighted versions of the Bible is acknowledged with appreciation:

Scripture references marked AMP are taken from the Amplified Bible, Copyright © 1954, 1958, 1962, 1964, 1965, 1987 by The Lockman Foundation. Used by permission.

Scripture references marked NLT are taken from the Holy Bible, *New Living Translation,* copyright © 1996, 2004 by Tyndale Charitable Trust. Used by permission of Tyndale House Publishers, Wheaton, Illinois 60189. All rights reserved.

Scripture references marked NIV are taken from the Holy Bible, *New International Version*®, NIV®. Copyright © 1973, 1978, 1984 by the International Bible Society. Used by permission of Zondervan. All rights reserved.

Scripture references marked TM are taken from *The Message Bible* © 1993 by Eugene N. Peterson, NavPress, PO Box 35001, Colorado Springs, CO 80935, 4th printing in USA 1994. Published in association with the literary agency—Alive Comm. PO Box 49068, Colorado Springs, CO 80949. Used by permission.

Scripture references marked CEV are taken from *The Contemporary English Version:* Thomas Nelson, 1997, c1995 by the American Bible Society. Used by permission. All rights reserved.

ISBN 13: 978-1-4141-1075-2
ISBN 10: 1-4141-1075-8
Library of Congress Catalog Card Number: 2006908388

What others are saying

About Kathy's first book, *Let's Talk About Salvation*

"*Let's Talk About Salvation* explains salvation in bite-size portions. As we went through each chapter, my children were able to gradually and thoroughly understand what it means to be saved. As a home-schooling mom of four children of various grades, this book allowed all the children to participate in the questions and games despite the age differences."

—J. Coburn, Ohio Home-Schooler

"This book was crystal clear on salvation. It helped me go over important biblical principles I was not covering as a parent. I loved how scripture backed up everything that was explained in the book. My child loved answering all the questions and couldn't wait till we read more. This book was easy to understand and enjoyable for me and my child."

—G. Matthews

"I think the best feature of this book is the section on questions for parent/teacher and children in the Think About it sections. It

gives them an opportunity to share their heart and answer questions that challenge their faith."
—S. Hayek, Christian Grade School Teacher

This book should be in every home and a part of every Sunday school program. Not only is it biblically sound, but it is fun and easy to read. This book was so thorough in its explanation of salvation that it could be used to lead any person to Christ but simple enough that my three-year-old was able to understand it. It helped me explain salvation to my children in a way that made sense to them. As we read each chapter together we were able to discuss how the material applied to them. I believe my children have a deeper understanding of what it means to be saved as a result of reading this book."
—K. Davis, Awana Leader

"This is a great book about salvation. We want our children to keep God's Word in their hearts. This book has great questions and games to play to help any unsaved parent understand more of what their children need to learn about God."
—K. Trice, Home-Schooler

"This book is a method for teaching young children in very simple terms how to give their lives to the Lord. It touches on major points concerning salvation."
—F. Dents

Contents

Acknowledgments......................................ix
A Message to Parents..................................xi
How to Use This Book................................xiii
Introduction..xvii

1. Jesus Our Savior 1
2. Jesus Our Lord 7
3. God Rules Rock! 13
4. God Is #1.. 19
5. One Special Day 27
6. Don't Tell Me What to Do 33
7. The Do Not Commandments 41
8. More Do Not Commandments 47
9. It Is Not About Me 53
10. It's Hard to Obey God's Rules 59
11. Jesus Our Helper 65
12. Jesus Our Miracle Worker........................ 73
13. Jesus Our Best Friend 79
14. Take a Look at Your Friends 85
15. Getting to Know Jesus........................... 93
16. What Happens When I Don't Know Jesus?........ 99

17. Jesus Our Everything 105
18. Jesus Our Heart. 115
19. Jesus Our Guide 123
20. Hanging Out with Jesus 131
21. Calling Our Best Friend 137
22. Dialing the Right Number. 143
23. Why Isn't Jesus Answering My Call? 149
24. I Can't Hear Jesus 155
25. Answer Key. 163

Acknowledgments

My thanks to God, who poured into me the content for this series of books and for using me as a vessel.

I couldn't have done this without the help of my friends and children who read it numerous times before its completion. A special thanks to my eight-year-old son, Cameron, who provided valuable insight.

I want to acknowledge all of the parents who are being intentional in their children's spiritual development.

I would like to dedicate this book to a dear friend, Brenda Winslow, who passed last year. God gave her the vision for this series even prior to sharing it with me. I shared with her the outline for my first book, *Let's Talk About Salvation*, which I thought would be the first and the last book, and she revealed to me that God wanted me to make this a series of books. I laughed when she said that, but when I finished the book a year later, I realized this was too much material for one book. I remembered what she said, and I began to write a series. I thank God that He used her to speak this idea into my life and help me be obedient to His will for this series.

A Message to Parents

This book is designed to encourage parents and children ages 7-12 to develop a relationship with God and to study the Word of God together. This is not a book for kids to read alone! Parents often attend Bible studies, read the Bible, or talk to Christian friends to learn more about God, but leave their children's growth to the church. The church only gets a few hours on the weekend to share the gospel with your children. What are they getting the other six days of the week?

As parents, our main job is to minister to our family. What better person to share the gospel with your children than you? If you do not lead your children to Christ, someone else will lead him or her away from Christ. As Dr. Randy Carlson, a Christian psychologist, says, "We need to be intentional parents." Intentional parents are those who are taking the lead in their children's spiritual development. It is never too early to teach your children about God. The best way to teach your children is to lead by example.

In our world today, the lines are blurred between Christians and non-Christians. No one knows who is or isn't a Christian because the majority of Christians look just like the world. Romans 12:2 tell us, *"Do not copy the behaviors and customs of this world, but let God transform you into a new person by changing the way you think"*

(NLT). It is important that parents paint the correct picture of what God expects from us and not the watered-down version. God will reward parents who use their abilities to raise godly children.

To raise godly children, you must act godly as well. Your children will imitate your behavior whether it is good or bad. They will learn what it means to be a Christian by what you do if you claim to be saved. Will your behavior cause them to sin or obey God? Matthew 18:6 tells us, *"But if anyone causes one of these little ones who believe in me to sin, it would be better for him to have a large millstone hung around his neck and to be drowned in the depths of the sea"* (NIV). What are you doing or not doing that will cause your children to sin? Are you going to church regularly, forgiving others, exhibiting the fruit of the spirit, using wholesome words and obeying God completely?

These books are designed to help parents grow along with their children. My children have asked many questions during this study, so I have put my answers to their questions and many others on my web site. Visit www.MyChildsHeart.org to find answers to commonly asked questions. I pray this series will be a blessing for you and your family.

How to Use This Book

This book will help parents and children realize they are under God's authority and how to make Jesus a friend. I encourage you to set aside time to read this book daily. God tells us that we should meditate on His Word day and night. What better way to start your day? You can set aside fifteen minutes in the morning to take turns reading, or read it at the dinner table during family dinner. My family takes turns reading each paragraph and answering the questions at dinner time, and this has been a lot of fun. You can also add this to your bedtime routine. It doesn't matter when you do it—just do it.

This book is divided into twenty-four devotions. Read one devotional daily. At the end of each devotional, answer the "**Think About It**" questions. They will help you think about what you have read and how it fits into your life. The parent questions are designed to demonstrate to your children that you had and have similar experiences and challenges. Please be mindful of your children's ages and only share age-appropriate things. This is not the time to air your dirty laundry. A "**Key Verse**" has been listed to help you remember what you have read. The **Key Verse** will help you obey God, remember how awesome God is, or help you not be afraid. "**Prayer Time**" is the time set aside for you to talk to God. Each devotion has a short prayer about what you have read. Please feel free to add more to this prayer. This is the time that you share everything with God.

After each **Think About It**, you will find a **Bible Quiz** and fun activity. This section is fun because you will have games to play to help you remember what you have read.

Parents and children can challenge each other in the **Bible Quiz** section to see who knows the most. Read your sections every day so you will be able to do the fun sections together.

I have found that it is easier to stay focused on God when I surround myself with those who will hold me accountable. This book is great for book clubs, Sunday school, and classrooms. Start a book club with other children and parents and meet once a week—or after the completion of the book—to discuss the material. My web site, www.MyChildsHeart.org, has group discussion questions and fun activities for each book. Allow at least two hours to fully answer the questions and to allow the children time to mingle and share their experiences with God. A small group will help you and your children to establish relationships with those who are trying to please God.

How to Use This Book

It is easier for children to follow Christ when they know that they are not alone. You want to establish a long-term relationship with those who are seeking God seriously. To continue developing devoted Christians, I am completing a series of books that can be read by your book club. So look for new books on our website (www.MyChildsHeart.org).

Introduction

Some of you are probably thinking, *Do I have to do anything special now that I am saved?* The answer is, yes, you do.

Do you remember when you started kindergarten? You were probably excited and frightened at the same time. You knew that you would have to learn new things and stop doing baby things. You probably even had to make new friends. I would guess you probably met one of your best friends in kindergarten. When you got to kindergarten, there was a lot to learn, but you learned it all. Then you moved to first grade and learned some more. Well, this is how it is when you become saved.

God wants you to start learning all about Him and be more like Christ. He wants to become your closest friend. The good thing is that you do not have to learn it all in one day. Just like school, you learn a little bit at a time. Every year you should be learning more and more. You cannot stop learning about God. I am in my forties, and I still learn more and more about God each day.

> For my determined purpose is that I may know Him, that I may progressively become more deeply and intimately acquainted with Him, perceiving and recognizing and understanding the wonders of His person.
>
> (Phil. 3:10, Amplified Bible)

My Child's Heart Series #2

This book is designed to help answer the following questions and more:

I'm saved, now what?

How do I make Jesus Lord?

Why does God have rules for me to follow?

What is Jesus like?

How can I be like Jesus?

How can Jesus be my friend?

Why is it important to be like Jesus?

How does God talk to me?

When can I talk to Jesus?

Does Jesus hear me when I talk to Him?

Chapter 1

Jesus Our Savior

In my book, *Let's Talk About Salvation*, I talked about how we are all sinners and need to be saved. It was Adam and Eve's sin that made all of us sinners. God told Adam and Eve that they could eat from all the trees in the garden but not from the tree of good and evil. Have you ever had your parents to tell you that you couldn't have that delicious chocolate cake on the table? Because they told you not to eat it; you probably wanted to eat it even more. Sometimes, do you go ahead and have the cake, even though you know it is wrong? Well, this is what Adam and Eve did. They sinned because Satan tricked Eve into believing that she would be like God if she ate the forbidden fruit. Sometimes, we believe Satan's lies and do wrong things that lead to bad consequences. Eve believed his lie, and she ate the fruit. She then gave the fruit to Adam to eat, and he did. Their terrible mistake of eating the fruit from the forbidden tree affects all of us today. Because of their sin, we are all sinners. We have to be saved to get to heaven. Jesus says in John 14:6a, "*I am the way and truth and the life. No one comes to the Father except through me*" (NIV).

You know you are saved when you do the following:

My Child's Heart Series #2

Believe and confess that Jesus is Lord and Savior. We have to believe in our hearts and say out loud to someone that Jesus is God. *"So you will be saved, if you honestly say, 'Jesus is Lord,' and if you believe with all your heart that God raised him from death. God will accept you and save you, if you truly believe this and tell it to others"* (Rom. 10:9-10, CEV).

Confess and Repent. The Bible tells us in 1 John 1:9(NIV), *"If we confess our sins, he is faithful and just and will forgive us our sins and purify us from all unrighteousness."*

Confess means to:

- A: Admit that your sin is wrong and that it is not pleasing to God.
- B: To tell God about the bad things you have done and ask for forgiveness.

Repent means to:

- A: Turn away from your sin.
- B: To be sorry for what you have done.
- C: To promise not to do it again.

Jesus Our Savior

When we repent of our sins, we are telling God that we are going to try very, very hard not to do it again. You may make a mistake and do it again, but just ask God to forgive you and ask for His help to remind you that sin is displeasing to Him. If you keep on doing the same sin over and over again, you have not repented. Remember, repent means to *stop doing*.

Make Jesus Lord Over Your Life. We make Jesus Lord over our lives when we truly believe in Him. Knowing that Jesus is Lord and Savior is not enough. We must believe in Him. Believe means to **trust** and **obey**. *"God accepts those who obey his Law, but not those who simply hear it"* (Rom. 2:13, CEV). Only believing and confessing that Jesus Christ died on the cross will save us. Being good and doing what is right does not save us. But after we are saved, we must start doing what God tells us to do. This means doing things God's way. After we believe in God, He sends us the Holy Spirit to live within us. When we get the Holy Spirit, He helps us to do what is right and obey God. We have to be obedient to God's Word. The Holy Spirit within us pushes us to do what is right. We know we are saved when we are sad about doing wrong and want to stop!

Jesus is Lord over our lives when we do what He says in the Bible. Satan knows that Jesus is Lord and Savior, but he has not made Christ the Lord over his life. In fact, he is God's enemy. So Satan is not saved.

Stop and ask yourself if you have made Jesus the Lord over your life. You can pray this simple prayer to make sure.

Dear Jesus, I believe that you are the Son of God and that you died on the cross to forgive me of my sins. I know I am a sinner, and I can do nothing to make up for my sins, but you loved me enough to die on the cross in my place. Please forgive me of my past sins (name some of your sins). *Thank you for loving me. I pray that you will wash me clean today so that I will put you first in my life and do what you want and not what I want to do. I ask the Holy Spirit to come into my life and guide me in this new life of serving you. Amen.*

If you prayed this today, please fill in the date._____

Think About It

Parent/Teacher:

> Do you know Jesus as your Lord and Savior?
> Share how your life has changed now that you are saved.

Children:

> What concerns/fears do you have about being saved?
> Do you know Jesus as your Lord and Savior?
> Are you obedient to God's Word?
> How do we prove that we are saved?

Key Verse

> For merely listening to the law doesn't make us right with God. It is obeying the law that makes us right in his sight.
> (Rom. 2:13, NLT)

Prayer Time

> *Dear Lord, please help me understand what it means to be a Christian. Help me to act like you each day. Amen.*

Jesus Our Savior

BIBLE QUIZ #1

Challenge your parents or sibling and see who can answer the most questions below correctly. Don't look at the answers below until you have finished.

1. What was the name of Adam and Eve's third son? (Gen. 5:3)
    a. Cain
    b. Abel
    c. Seth

2. How old was Adam when he died? (Gen. 5:5)
    a. 930 years old
    b. 600 years old
    c. 800 years old

3. God created the world in ____ days and rested on ____ day. (Gen. 1:27-2:3)

4. Why did God kick Adam and Eve out of the garden? (Gen. 3:22-23)

5. Complete: For God so loved the world that he gave his only begotten Son, that whosoever believeth in him should not perish but have_____.(John 3:16)

Answer: 1. Seth, 2. 930, 3. 6 days, 7 days, 4. They ate from the tree of good and evil, 5. Eternal life.

My Child's Heart Series #2

Fun Time #1

How many words can you and your parents make from the word below? (You should be able to find at least sixteen words.)

Salvation

saint
_____   _____

_____   _____

_____   _____

_____   _____

_____   _____

_____   _____

_____   _____

_____   _____

_____   _____

_____   _____

Chapter 2
Jesus Our Lord

Being saved, or what we call a "Christian," is so awesome. We are now a part of God's family. In families each person has a key role. You probably have some responsibilities like taking out the trash, keeping your room clean, or washing the dishes. Even though you are young, your role in the family is important. You also have an important role in God's family. Your role is to show others Him. We show others God by believing and trusting in Him. We show others God by making Him Lord over our lives. This means doing what He says in the Bible.

    Do not talk or run in the halls. No eating in the classroom or talking with food in your mouth. What are these? You are correct if you said *rules*. Your school, parents, and the city have rules. No one likes rules, but they are here to protect us. Imagine what your classroom would be like without rules. I'm sure many of you are probably thinking it would be fun. But let me paint a realistic picture for you. Children would talk all of the time and disrupt class, which means the teacher could not teach and you would not learn anything. This probably sounds okay to some, but staying in the same grade for years probably would get boring and embarrassing after awhile.

My Child's Heart Series #2

Mary and her mom were extremely poor. They barely had enough money to buy food. One day, a servant of the king came and requested the monthly tithe. A tithe is 10% of all the money a family makes. Mary couldn't understand why they had to give their food money to the king. Her mom told her that the king was in charge, and he could make whatever rules he wanted. And they had to obey his rules. Mary said, "But mom, if we give him this money, we will not be able to eat for days." Her mom replied, "If we do not give him the money, he will punish us by throwing us in jail, and that would be worse than us going without food."

Everybody in the world has to follow some type of rule. We might not like It, but rules are here to protect us.

God is our Lord and King, and He has rules as well. His rules are made to protect us. As a part of God's family, we have to follow His rules. When we accept Jesus as our Lord and Savior, we are telling God that we will obey all of His rules.

Jesus Our Lord

Since God made us, we belong to Him to do His will. We have to do what He tells us to do in the Bible. Let's say you are the owner of a brand new puppy. The puppy has to do what you tell him to do. You would be a bad owner if you didn't teach your dog to not run into the street. As a good owner, you would not leave your dog loose in the backyard without a fence. If you did, he could wander off and get lost, someone could take him, or someone could hurt him. Well, God's rules are kind of like the fence. When we obey His rules, we will not get lost, stolen from Him by Satan, or hurt by Satan and others.

God has written all of His rules in the Bible. The Bible shows us right from wrong and good from bad. When we accept God as our Lord and Savior, we accept all of God's rules.

Think About It

Parent/Teacher:

> Discuss how you have made Jesus Lord over your life.
> How is your life better now that Jesus is Lord over your life?

Children:

> What does it mean to make Jesus Lord over your life?
> How can you show people that God is Lord over your life?

Key Verse

> And anyone who believes in God's Son has eternal life. Anyone who doesn't obey the Son will never experience eternal life but remains under God's angry judgment."
>
> (John 3:36, NLT)

Prayer Time

> *Dear God, please help me to make you Lord over my life. Help me to believe that I must do what you say. Amen.*

Jesus Our Lord

Bible Quiz #2

Challenge your parents or sibling and see who can answer the most questions below correctly. Don't look at the answers below until you have finished.

1. Which Old Testament book tells about Abraham?

2. Goliath was a friend of Saul. True or False (1 Sam. 17:4)

3. Joseph was twenty-five when his brothers sold him into slavery. True or False (Gen. 37:2)

4. Esau sold his birthright for—. (Gen. 25:34)
    a. New clothing
    b. A sheep
    c. A bowl of stew

5. Who did Isaac bless instead of Esau? (Gen. 27:21-23)

Answers: 1. Genesis, 2. False, 3. False, 4. A bowl of stew, 5. Jacob

FUN TIME #2

Write out the statement below using the number grid. Each number has a matching letter.

A	B	C	D	E	F	G	H	I	J	K	L	M
1	2	3	4	5	6	7	8	9	10	11	12	13

N	O	P	Q	R	S	T	U	V	W	X	Y	Z
14	15	16	17	18	19	20	21	22	23	24	25	26

_____ _____
2 5 12 9 5 22 5   20 8 1 20

_____ _____
10 5 19 21 19   9 19

_____ _____
12 15 18 4   1 14 4

_____
19 1 22 9 15 18

Chapter 3
God Rules Rock!

The Ten Commandments are a set of God's rules. We accept these rules in our salvation agreement. They were given to us to show us how to love God and other people. God gave us His Son to show how much He loves us. By obeying the Ten Commandments, we show Jesus how much we love Him. "*But those who obey God's word truly show how completely they love him. That is how we know we are living in him*" (1 John 2:5, NLT).

God loves us so much that He wants to protect us from ourselves, others, and Satan. He gave us the Bible, which has many rules. We are going to look at the Ten Commandments, which are rules that help us to love others and God. Learning the Ten Commandments is as important as learning your ABCs. You have to know your ABCs to read, and you have to know the Ten Commandments to obey God. They protect us and show us right from wrong. God gave us the Ten Commandments because of His love for us. He wants what is best for us. The Ten Commandments are not suggestions but commands. He expects and demands that we obey them.

Jesus said in Matthew 5:19, "*Anyone who breaks one of the least of these commandments and teaches others to do the same will be called least in the kingdom of heaven, but whoever practices and teaches these commands will be called great in the kingdom of heaven*" (NIV).

My Child's Heart Series #2

Funny Rock Jokes:

What do you call a dog that collects rocks?
What does a rock want to be when it grows up?
What is a rock's favorite cereal?

Megan's friends were talking about how they wished they had a computer game like Emily's. They thought Emily was so cool and blessed because her parents got her this game. All day they talked about it. Finally, Megan got sick of it and told them that God says that we should not covet other people's things—in other words want something badly that belongs to another. Megan said, "This is one of the Ten Commandments." All of her friends began to laugh. One of her friends said, "That is old news, we only have to do the things in the New Testament." Another friend said, "The Ten Commandments were only for the Israelites."

Some people might tell you the Ten Commandments are not for Christians today but that is an untruth. In Matthew 5:17, Jesus says, *"Do not think that I came to abolish the Law (ten commandments) or the Prophets; I did not come to abolish, but to fulfill"* (NASB).

God Rules Rock!

Think About It

Parent/Teacher:

> Share rules that you must follow. Tell what will happen if you disobey them.
> What rules do you have a problem obeying?

Children:

> What will happen to those who disobey God's commandments?
> Why is it important to obey God's rules?
> When we obey God, what are we telling Him?
> What rules do you have a problem obeying?
> What are two things that you do that are pleasing to God?

Key Verse

> If you love me, you will obey what I command.
> (John 14:15, NIV)

Prayer Time

> *Dear God, thank you for your rules. Please help me realize that your rules are important, and help me to follow them. Amen.*

My Child's Heart Series #2

BIBLE QUIZ #3

Challenge your parents or sibling and see who can answer the most questions below correctly. Don't look at the answers below until you have finished.

1. Who interpreted Pharaoh's dream? (Gen. 41:25)

2. Faith without _____ is dead? (James 2:20)

3. Who was the first king of Israel? (1 Sam. 10:21-25)
    a. David
    b. Samson
    c. Saul

4. What is Moses' sister's name? (Ex. 4:14, 15:20)
    a. Miriam
    b. Ruth
    c. Gabriel

5. Who were the parents of King Solomon? (1 Kings 1:11-13)

Answers: 1. Joseph, 2. Works, 3. Saul, 4. Miriam, 5. David and Bathsheba

God Rules Rock!

Fun Time #3

God has many rules for us because He created the world. I want you and your parents to create a new world and write down the rules for this new world. Feel free to draw a picture. Share your world with one another when you are done. Include the following in your description of the new world:

1. Think about things that you don't like in our world and make changes to them.

2. Think about how you will make men and women (will we be like super heroes or just like we are now).

3. How will we travel (cars that fly or drive on the street)?

4. Will we have schools like today?

Chapter 4

God Is #1

God created us and owns us. He has the right to tell us how He wants to be treated. He wants us to love Him. The love that you have for your parents is the same type of love that God wants. The first three commandments show us how to worship and love God.

> You shall have no other gods before me.
> (Ex. 20:3, NIV)

No one should be more important than God. Not even yourself. Who is most important to you? Is it your friend at school, someone on television, the person who sings your favorite song, a girl or boy, your games or sports? God wants to be number one in your life. If you think about anything else more than God, He is not number one.

God needs to be first in our lives. I love my family, but I cannot put them before God. I have great friends, but I cannot put them before God. I love walking, but I cannot put this before God. All of these things are okay, but they must not be more important than God.

We show God that He is number one when we obey Him, read the Bible, and pray every day. God is number one when we don't

My Child's Heart Series #2

let anything stop us from going to church every week. God is number one when we care more about what He thinks than what our friends think.

> You shall not make for yourself an idol in the form of anything in heaven above or on the earth beneath or in the waters below.
> (Ex. 20:4, NIV)

You must worship only the Lord, not your parents, not a friend, not a movie star or sports hero, not a car or boat or skateboard. We were made to worship God only. Worship means to honor, love without any questions, admire, and to devote a lot of time to. If we are not worshipping God, we will worship something or someone else. We sometimes make other things more important than God, most often ourselves. When we do what we want to do regardless of what the Bible tells us, we are putting ourselves before God.

God Is #1

Jonathan loves to make his friends laugh. He thinks they like him because he is funny. One day while they were in the classroom, he wanted them to think that he was cool. So he decided to pull the chair from under Rachel as she sat down. She hit the floor hard. All the kids began to laugh. Jonathan felt really bad about hurting her, but he still was glad that he made his friends laugh. All the boys thought he was cool. God sees everything that we do, and He was not proud of Jonathan's behavior. In this case, Jonathan put himself and his friends ahead of God because God tells us to love everyone and treat them better than we treat ourselves.

> You shall not misuse the name of the LORD your God, for the LORD will not hold anyone guiltless who misuses his name.
> (Ex. 20:7, NIV)

You should not swear. You may sometimes hear someone say, "I am telling the truth, I swear to God." Many people use God's name like a swear word, or say it when they're upset. God wants us to use His name when we're talking to Him or telling others about Him in a nice way. To use His name in these other ways is very disrespectful and hurts God's feelings.

Did You Know?

Charles Lindbergh: 1st man to fly solo across the Atlantic in 1927.
Kathryn Sullivan: 1st female US astronaut to walk in space 1984.
Victoria Woodhall: 1st woman to run for President of the US in 1872.
Charles Curtis: 1st American Indian to become a US Senator (Kansas) in 1907
Carol Elizabeth Moseley-Braun: 1st Black woman in US Senate 1993.
Hattie Caraway: 1st woman elected to US Senate 1932.
Charles Cooper: 1st Black player in NBA (Fort Wayne Indiana Celtics) in 1950.

Neil Armstrong: 1st man to walk on the moon in 1969.
Colin Powell: 1st Black Secretary of State in 2000.
Antonia Novello: 1st woman and first Hispanic to be named Surgeon General of the US 1990.

God Is #1

THINK ABOUT IT

Parent/Teacher:

> How do you show that God is first in your life?
> Is it hard to put God first in your life?

Children:

> What do you think are the greatest things about God?
> What ways can you show that God is first in your life?
> What will you start doing to show God that He is number one in your life?

Key Verse

> Worship the LORD with gladness; come before him with joyful songs.
>
> (Ps. 100:2, NIV)

Prayer Time

> *Dear God, thank you for loving me. I want to show you that I love you. Help me to put you first in my life. Amen.*

Bible Quiz #4

Challenge your parents or sibling and see who can answer the most questions below correctly. Don't look at the answers below until you have finished.

1. When a person uses the names God, Lord, or Jesus Christ and they are not praying or talking to some one about them, they are _____ ?
   a. Doing nothing wrong
   b. Just playing around so there is no harm
   c. Using the Lord's names in vain

2. If a person were to say to you "Thou shalt not take the name of the LORD thy God in vain" they would be referring to the _____ commandment?
   a. Second
   b. First
   c. Third

3. "Thou shalt have no other gods before me" is which commandment?
   a. Second
   b. First
   c. Third

4. When we have troubles in life, we should turn to _____ for help.
   a. Your friends
   b. An idol
   c. God

5. An idol is _____ .
   a. Someone or something more important than God
   b. A carving in wood or stone that some people worship
   c. All of the above

Answers: 1. Using the Lord's Names in vain, 2. Third, 3. First, 4. God, 5. All of the above

God Is #1

Fun Time #4

Across

1. Who created us?
7. You shall not m_____e the Lord's name.
8. F_____ should not be put before God.
9. Sp_____ should not be put before God.
10. Saying, "Oh my God" is using the Lord's name in v_____.

Down

2. You shall have no _____ gods before me.
3. The first three commandments show us how to _____ God.
4. Christians must put God _____ in their lives.
5. The Ten Commandments are God's r_____s.
6. We honor God by w_____g Him.

Chapter 5
One Special Day

Commandment four tells us the importance of setting aside a day for God and rest.

Remember to observe the Sabbath day by keeping it holy.
(Ex. 20:8, NIV)

God created the entire world and man in six days. He rested on the seventh day. Do you think our powerful God was tired? Not at all, He rested to show us the importance of resting. God knows that it is very tiring to go to school, play sports, and do all of our other activities. This is why He tells us to rest on the seventh day. If your parents didn't tell you to go to sleep at night, you would probably stay up very late. How well do you think you would do in school if you stayed up to midnight every night? You probably would fall asleep in class and be very dumb.

Well, God knows how much we like to have fun and do a lot of things, so He tells us to rest on the seventh day. This commandment is telling us that God designed us to rest. Not only does God want us to rest, but He also wants us to set aside a day to worship Him. The day that you do this is not important. Some people go to church on Saturday and others on Sunday. Being in activities is great, but God wants us to set aside one day for Him and the church. It is important that we spend time around those who serve and love God.

In Luke 10:38-42 (NIV), Jesus tells His friend Mary that she is focusing on the wrong thing. "*As Jesus and his disciples were on their way, he came to a village where a woman named Martha opened her home to him. She had a sister called Mary, who sat at the Lord's feet listening to what he said. But Martha was distracted by all the preparations that had to be made. She came to him and asked, 'Lord, don't you care that my sister has left me to do the work by myself? Tell her to help me!' 'Martha, Martha,' the Lord answered, 'you are worried and upset about many things, but only one thing is needed. Mary has chosen what is better and it will not be taken away from her.'*"

Martha was so busy cleaning and preparing a meal, but Jesus wanted her to be near Him and listen to His Words. Don't be too busy to spend time with God. Put Him first!

One Special Day

When you attend Sunday school or church, please pay attention. Satan will tell you that church is dumb. Your mind will wander off to the fun things that you want to do after church. You may even have other children distracting you. When you get to heaven, God is going to ask you why didn't you go to church and why didn't you listen. Everything your teacher or pastor is telling you is to help you live a better life. So pay attention!

Think About It

Parent/Teacher:

> How well are you recognizing the Sabbath?
> Discuss your children's activities and determine if they are getting enough time to rest, spend time with family, and God.

Children:

> What activities do you think God wants you to do on the Sabbath?
> Do you feel like you are involved in too many activities?
> What did Martha do that was wrong?

Key Verse

> Six days you shall labor, but on the seventh day you shall rest
> (Ex. 34:21, NIV)

Prayer Time

> *Dear God, you are important. Please help me to spend time with you and rest. Amen.*

One Special Day

Bible Quiz #5

Challenge your parents or sibling and see who can answer the most questions below correctly. Don't look at the answers below until you have finished.

1. What day is the Sabbath day?
   a. Saturday
   b. Sunday
   c. Jesus Christ has become our Sabbath

2. Who lived longer than anyone in the Bible? (Gen. 5:20)

3. Who did God promise to make their descendants like the dust of the earth? (Gen. 13:16)
   a. Abraham
   b. Joseph
   c. David

4. Who is Seth's father? (Gen. 4:25)

5. Who is Noah's father? (Gen. 5:29)

Answers: 1. Jesus Christ has become our Sabbath, 2. Methuselah, 3. Abraham, 4. Adam, 5. Lamech

FUN TIME #5

List all the fun things you can do as a family together on the Sabbath. Share these with your parents.

_____

_____

_____

_____

_____

_____

_____

_____

Chapter 6
Don't Tell Me What to Do

If you do not like being told what to do, that is too bad. Welcome to the wonderful world of being a Christian. No one said, "This is going to be easy." God expects us to obey Him even when it is hard. I don't like people telling me what to do, but I know that God has put certain people in authority over me and I must listen to them. As a wife, God has put my husband in authority over me. So I must listen to what He says.

Well, God has given your parents authority over you. Authority means that they have the right to tell you what to do. God expects your parents to help you do what is right. God commands children to do what their parents tell them in commandment five.

> Respect your father and mother, and you will live a long and successful life in the land I am giving you.
> (Deut. 5:16, CEV)

Has your mom or dad ever asked you for a helping hand or to do something? Have you noticed how good things go when you do as they ask? There is a reason for that. The fifth commandment is so important because it is the only commandment with a promise. When you obey your parents, God promises you a long and successful life.

Respect means to obey and love your parents. If you fail to obey and love your mother and father, you could be cutting yourself off from God's blessings.

Respecting your parents means doing what they say whether you like it or not, provided that it does not go against the Word of God. The Bible doesn't say obey them only when you want to or only when it is something you want to do. It says, "Obey at all times." By learning how to obey your parents, you are learning how to obey God. You are obeying Him when you obey your parents.

When your parents tell you to do something or not to do something, you must do it even when they are not around. Some children obey their parents when they are around but when they are not around they do things that are wrong. Remember your parents may not be there, but God is watching everything you do.

Don't Tell Me What to Do

God told the Israelites to march around the walls of Jericho seven times. This probably sounded pretty dumb to them, but they did it anyway. Your parents' rules may seem dumb, but you must obey them as the Israelites obeyed God. Because the Israelites marched around the walls of Jericho, God blessed them and they won the war. God will bless you also when you obey your parents.

You can also show respect or disrespect to your parents in the way you communicate to them. Communication can be in the form of talking, listening, and body movements. How is your attitude when your parents tell you what to do or correct you? Are you rolling your eyes, not listening, or talking back? Do you immediately do what your parents ask you or do you continue to do what you want to do? When your parents ask you to clean up, do you argue or grumble? God says, "This is a sin." By doing this you are not respecting authority.

If you have a problem honoring your parents, confess this sin to your parents and God and ask God to help you. Also start saying every day Ephesians 6:1:"*Children, obey your parents in the Lord, for this is right*" (NIV).

You disrespect your parents when....

> You wait to do what they tell you to do.
> You don't do what they tell you to do.
> You lie to them.
> You talk bad about them to others.
> You complain when they tell you what to do.
> You talk back to them.
> You stomp up the stairs after they tell you to do something.
> You don't keep your room clean after they have asked you to do so.
> You don't do your chores correctly or when they are supposed to be done.
> You call your parents stupid or some other name when they don't let you do what you want.

Brianna was out at the shopping mall with her friends. Her mom told her to be home by 5 P.M. for dinner. She looked at her watch and it was 4:45 and it took her 15 minutes to get home. She told her friends that she had to leave to be home on time. They told her that eating dinner with her family was dumb. They explained that they never ate with their families. She felt like a loser, so she ignored her mother and continued to have fun for another thirty minutes. When she arrived home, her family had finished dinner. Her father punished her for being disobedient. She didn't think this was fair because none of her friends had to do it.

Brianna was being disobedient. It doesn't matter whether you think your parents are fair. You still have to obey them. Brianna needs to find friends that will encourage her to do the right thing rather than make fun of her.

You might not agree with what your parents are telling you, and you might feel that they are being unfair, but you have to obey them. When you obey your parents; you are showing God you love Him. And you do love God, don't you!

Don't Tell Me What to Do

Think About It

Parent/Teacher:

> Share with your children how they are doing with obeying and respecting you. Please be specific so they can learn from this conversation.
>
> Put a plan together to help them improve in this area. Start by having them memorize the key verse and recite it daily. Ask them how you can help them be more obedient.

Children:

> On a scale of one (one is poor) to ten (all the time), how well do you respect and obey your parents?
>
> How can you show respect to your parents?
>
> Is it a sin to disobey your parents?
>
> What did God say will happen to those who obey their parents?
>
> Talk about when and why it is difficult to obey your parents.

Key Verse

> Children, obey your parents in the Lord, for this is right.
>
> (Eph. 6:1, NIV)

Prayer Time

> *Dear God, please help me to understand the importance of obeying my parents. Help me to know that disobedience is a sin and does not please you. Please help me obey them even when I don't want to. Amen.*

My Child's Heart Series #2

BIBLE QUIZ #6

Challenge your parents or sibling and see who can answer the most questions below correctly. Don't look at the answers below until you have finished.

1. Lazarus had been in the tomb for three days before Jesus arrived. True or False (John 11:17)

2. Who is Jacob's father? (Gen. 25:21-27)

3. King Herod gave the head of John the Baptist to his wicked wife. True or False (Matt. 14:6-11)

4. "Honor thy father and thy mother" is which commandment?
   a. Fourth
   b. Fifth
   c. Seventh

5. What is Moses' brother's name? (Ex. 4:14).
   a. Aaron
   b. Jacob
   c. Stephen

Answers: 1. True, 2. Isaac, 3. False, 4. Fifth, 5. Aaron

Don't Tell Me What to Do

Fun Time #6

Unscramble the Bible verse Deuteronomy 5:16 to see what happens when you obey your parents.

| _____ | _____ | _____ | _____ |
| tcepseR | ruoy | rehtaf | dna |

| _____ | _____ | _____ | _____ |
| rehtom | dna | uoy | lliw |

| _____ | _____ | _____ | _____ |
| evil | a | gnol | dna |

| _____ | _____ | _____ | _____ |
| lufsseccus | efil | ni | eht |

| _____ | _____ | _____ | _____ |
| dnal | I | ma | gnivig |

| _____ |
| uoy |

Chapter 7
The Do Not Commandments

The last five commandments are the "do not" commands. God expects us to love one another and to put others first, and these commandments help us to do just that.

Do not murder.

(Ex. 20:13, NLT)

God created all of us and thinks we are all very special. So He forbids us from taking someone else's life. I'm sure you are probably thinking that you would never murder someone, and you are probably right. But Jesus tells us that we can also murder someone by what we say. He does not want us to destroy others with our words. We should always be careful with our words. Never repeat rumors. Do not tell lies about others. Do not gossip about someone or say nasty mean things to someone. What we say can hurt someone terribly. You know what I mean. It is how you feel when someone says something unkind to you.

You're familiar with the command to the ancients, "Do not murder." I'm telling you that anyone who is so much as angry with a brother or sister is guilty of murder. Carelessly call a brother "idiot!" and you just might find yourself hauled into court. Thoughtlessly yell "stupid!" at a sister and you are on the brink of hellfire. The simple moral fact is that words kill.

(Matt. 5:21-22, MSG)

Some Hurtful Words Are....

You are stupid, ugly, dumb
Sarah parents got a divorce
Mike got a "D" on his test
I'm smarter than you
I don't want you on my team because you can't play

Do not commit adultery.

(Ex. 20:14, NLT)

This is mostly for married people. He wants us to love our wife or husband and treat them with respect. When people aren't married, this commandment reminds us to be a true friend. Do not break promises. Do not lead our friends to break their promises.

Do not steal.

(Ex. 20:15, NLT)

We steal when we take something that doesn't belong to us. We are to be happy and satisfied with what God has given us. He wants us to come to Him for all of our needs and be patient for Him to give us the things we want, if it is His will. There are things that we want that God doesn't think we should have. So He does not give us everything we want.

How do you feel when someone takes something of yours? Thinking about how you would feel if someone stole from you will help you be honest with others. Loving God means that we will "look before we leap." When we see something we want, we will make sure it is ours to take! We will make sure we are doing the right thing. No excuses!

Jacob was so excited when he saw David's new Gameboy © game. They played with it for hours. He wanted one just like his. In fact, he asked David to let him borrow it for the weekend. When

The Do Not Commandments

he had to take it back on Monday, he told David that he had lost it. He hadn't really lost it. He just couldn't give it back because he loved it so. David was really sad to find out his new game was lost. He asked his parents for a new one but they told him no.

Jacob was so excited to get home that day to play with the game, but he knew he couldn't let his parents see it. So he hid under his bed and played it there. It wasn't all that comfortable, but at least he could play. Jacob eventually became bored playing the game under the bed. It is so much more fun to play with someone, but he couldn't let anyone know he had the game. This wasn't as much fun as he thought it would be. He was used to playing his games with David.

Jacob wanted to give the game back to David, but he didn't know how to do it. So he came up with another lie. He told David that he found his game under his bed. He felt bad about telling another lie. But he didn't want David to dislike him.

Jacob was coveting the game. He wanted the game so badly that he stole it. After he stole it he realized that it wasn't worth it. He lost a friend, and he felt terrible every day. Then he had to tell another lie to get out of the first lie. This is why it is so important to be satisfied with what you have.

Think About It

Parent/Teacher:

Share with your children how it makes you feel when someone steals something from you.
Share a time when someone did something that was hurtful.
Share how you felt about this person.

Children:

Share a time when someone did something that was hurtful.
Share two ways you have hurt others.
What kind of words can help people?
What kind of words can hurt people?

Key Verse

Love one another deeply, from the heart.
(1 Peter 1:22b, NIV)

Prayer Time

Dear God, thank you for blessing me with many things. Help me not to take something that belongs to someone else. Help me to love others and treat them the way I want to be treated. Amen.

The Do Not Commandments

Bible Quiz #7

Challenge your parents or sibling and see who can answer the most questions below correctly. Don't look at the answers below until you have finished.

1. Thou shall not commit adultery is what commandment?
   a. Sixth
   b. Fifth
   c. Seventh

2. What is the name of Saul's son who is David's friend? (1 Sam. 13:22)
   a. Jonathan
   b. Joseph
   c. Joel

3. "Thou shalt not kill" is the _____ commandment.
   a. Fourth
   b. Eight
   c. Sixth

4. How old was Joseph when his brothers sold him into slavery? (Gen. 37:2)

5. Who did Ruth marry after her first husband died? (Ruth 4:13)

Answers: 1. Seventh, 2. Jonathan, 3. Sixth, 4. Seventeen, 5. Boaz

My Child's Heart Series #2

Fun Time #7

Work with your parents to fill in the missing numbers. The missing numbers are between zero and five. The numbers in each row add up to totals to the right. The numbers in each column add up to the totals along the bottom. The diagonal lines also add up the totals to the right.

				13
1				12
	3			8
			1	12
	3	0	3	7
6	15	9	9	10

46

Chapter 8
More Do Not Commandments

Do not testify falsely against your neighbor.

(Ex. 20:16, NLT)

This commandment tells us to tell the truth. It is a sin to lie. We normally lie when we are afraid of making someone angry or getting into trouble. So don't do bad things, and you won't have to lie. Lies only hurt you and other people. You should make sure you do not add anything to the truth. You may think it makes you look special or cool to stretch the truth a bit, but it only makes you look bad. Telling tall tales or lies to others, even in fun, could make your friends not trust you or believe you even when you are telling the truth.

God is a God of truth, and He expects us to tell the truth. Most of the time, we lie for selfish reasons. We lie so that we will not be punished. We can't keep secrets from God! He knows everything and will make secrets known to others. Trying to hide will only get us into bigger trouble. When we are tempted to do wrong, we should ask Jesus to help us make the right choice. Then there will be no need to hide! The Holy Spirit is in us to help us do right.

My Child's Heart Series #2

A false witness will not go unpunished, nor will a liar escape.
(Prov. 19:5, NLT)

When you lie, the lie takes on a life of its own. It grows into this huge monster that is out of control. Satan tempted Eve with the fruit, and she ate it and then gave it to Adam to eat. When God questioned Adam and Eve about eating the fruit, Adam blamed it on Eve, and Eve blamed it on the Serpent.

Neither one took responsibility for their sin. Because sin brings shame and fear, we try to cover it up. Adam and Eve tried to cover up their nakedness with leaves, but God knows everything. This is what happens to us when we sin. If we steal something, we typically lie when questioned about it; we might even say that someone else stole it and then hide it until it is safe to bring out. Remember that God sees everything!

More Do Not Commandments

Do not covet

(Ex. 20:17, NLT)

This means that we shouldn't wish to have things that someone else has. Have you ever visited a friend and thought that their house was better than yours? Have you ever thought that your friend's parents are nicer than yours and wished they were yours? Have you ever wished that you looked like someone else or could be as smart as someone else? God does not want you to think about what you do not have. He wants you to be content with what He has given you. Content means being happy with what you have. Don't be a Mr. Want! Always wanting things can cause trouble. If you constantly want things that your parents say you cannot have, you might get angry with them or start feeling sorry for yourself because you don't have those things. These are bad feelings to have because they focus on you and not on God.

When we spend a lot of time thinking about what we don't have, we forget about God. Thinking about God will help you forget about what you don't have. Thinking about God will make you happy.

Did You Know?

An average pencil could draw a line thirty-five miles long if it were used right to the end without wasting any material in sharpening. The lead in today's pencils isn't lead at all, but graphite.

My Child's Heart Series #2

THINK ABOUT IT

Parent/Teacher:

Share a time that you lied and how it hurt you or someone else.

When have you wanted something that someone else had or to be someone else? How did this affect your attitude or feelings?

Children:

Share why you normally lie.

Share how you lied and got in trouble.

Share how you can keep from lying.

When have you wanted something that someone else had or to be someone else? (Maybe you wanted to be as smart as this person or play softball as well as this person.) How did this make you feel? What did you do?

Key Verse

There is nothing hidden that will not be found. There is no secret that will not be well known.

(Luke 8:17, CEV)

Prayer Time

Dear God, it is so easy to hurt others to protect myself. Help me not to do things that will hurt others. Help me to be satisfied with what I have. Amen.

More Do Not Commandments

BIBLE QUIZ #8

Challenge your parents or sibling and see who can answer the most questions below correctly. Don't look at the answers below until you have finished.

1. Your friend has everything you ever wanted. What do you do?
   a. Steal it from him when he is not looking.
   b. Be angry because you don't have everything you want.
   c. Be happy with what you do have.

2. Your teacher is looking for a classmate to help you with a special project. She has decided to pick from two people. One of the people is your best friend who doesn't always do her best and the other is someone whom you don't like but she normally does her best. Your teacher asks you which one would do a better job, so what do you say?
   a. Your friend is a better worker.
   b. The person you don't like is the better worker.

3. In what book of the Bible will you find the Ten Commandments?
   a. Genesis
   b. Exodus
   c. Leviticus

4. "Thou shalt not bear false witness against thy neighbour" is which commandment?
   a. Ninth
   b. Third
   c. Sixth

5. To whom did God give the Ten Commandments? (Ex. 19:24-20:1-21)
   a. Joseph
   b. Moses
   c. Abraham

Answers: 1. Be happy with what you do have, 2. The person you don't like is a better worker, 3. Exodus, 4. Ninth, 5. Moses

Fun Time #8

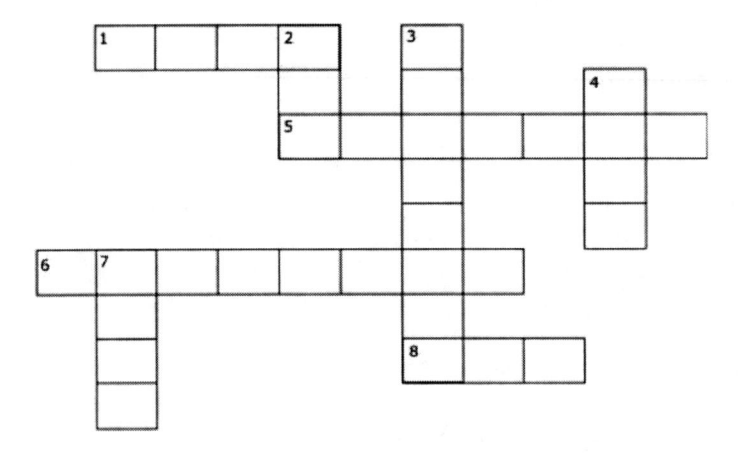

Across

1. Bad words will do this to a person.
5. God tells us to love our.
6. Whine about what you have to do.
8. He created all of us God.

Down

2. Not telling the truth.
3. Taking something that does not belong to you.
4. What we should do on the seventh day of the week.
7. Doing what God tell us to do.

Chapter 9
It Is Not About Me

Love your neighbor as yourself.

(Matt. 22:39b, NLT)

In the New Testament, Jesus gave us a new commandment to love our neighbor better than ourselves. Our neighbor is any person that we know or come in contact with. Wow, Jesus wants us to think about other people before we think about ourselves. This commandment is so awesome because it covers all of the Ten Commandments in one. If we did only this one, we would be keeping all the rest. When we love our brother, we will not steal, commit adultery, we will not kill, we will not lie on them, and we will not want what they have.

Who do you love now? Do you like only the people at school who are popular? Do you like only those who are pretty or wear cool clothing? Maybe you only like people with a certain skin color? Do you like only those who are nice to you? Do you like only those who like the things you like?

Well, God loves people no matter their skin color, no matter what they like or dislike and whether they're good or bad. And He expects us to do the same. God does not like it when people do bad things, and we shouldn't either, but He still loves them. God wants us to love other people the way He does. He wants us to show His love to others, just the way Jesus would. When we pray for others to be blessed by God, even when they have hurt us, we are showing love.

Ryan's younger brother always wanted to play with Ryan's toys. Ryan didn't mind him playing with them, but he would always break them. Ryan would get angry at his brother and hit him. His brother would be sent to time out but would continue to do it. Ryan couldn't understand why he gets into trouble for hitting his brother.

His mother would always say, "Your brother is younger, and we have to show him how to respect our things. God tells us to love one another and you are not being loving when you hit your brother. Romans 12:21 says, 'Don't let evil get the best of you; get the best of evil by doing good' (TM). So when your brother destroys your things, it is not your job to get him back. Tell him that this is not right and that you will not allow him to play with them if he continues. It is my job to punish your brother for his wrongdoing just like it is God's job to punish all of His children when they do

It Is Not About Me

wrong. Although God expects us to love others, He does not want us to allow people to hurt us and destroy our things."

Ryan understood what his mother was saying and tried to be loving towards his brother. After some time had passed, he realized that his brother was not changing. He was tired of forgiving his brother. He decided that he would never let his brother play with his things again no matter what.

When his mother realized that he had stopped playing with his younger brother, she asked to talk to him. She told him that God expects us to forgive each other and give each other second chances. Ryan said, "But Mom, I have forgiven him many times. How many times must I forgive him?" His mother pulled out her Bible and asked Ryan to read Matthew 18:21-22. It reads, *"Then Peter came and said to Him, 'Lord, how often shall my brother sin against me and I forgive him? Up to seven times?' Jesus said to him, 'I do not say to you, up to seven times, but up to seventy times seven'"* (NASB). So Ryan's mom asked, "Have you forgiven him 490 times?" Ryan replied, "Oh, Mom, I guess not. I will continue to forgive him because God continues to forgive me."

Paul tells us in 1 Corinthians 13:4-8: *"Love is kind and patient, never jealous, boastful, proud, or rude. Love isn't selfish or quick tempered. It doesn't keep a record of wrongs that others do. Love rejoices in the truth, but not in evil. Love is always supportive, loyal, hopeful, and trusting"* (CEV).

Think About It

Parent/Teacher:

Share how you can show love to someone who is difficult to get along with.

Children:

What can we do that will help us keep all the commandments? Share two things that you can do at school that will show your classmates love?

Key Verse

Dear friends, since God so loved us, we also ought to love one another.

(1 John 4:11, NIV)

Prayer Time

Dear God, I know that you love me no matter what I do. Help me show this same love to others. Help me to not just think about myself all of the time. Amen.

It Is Not About Me

Bible Quiz #9

Challenge your parents or sibling and see who can answer the most questions below correctly. Don't look at the answers below until you have finished.

1. God told Abraham that He is his… (Gen. 15:1)
   a. Buddy
   b. Friend
   c. Shield

2. How old was Abraham when he and Sarah had their first child? (Gen. 21:5)

3. How long did it rain during the flood? (Gen. 7:12)

4. How many books are in the New Testament?

5. What did God change Jacob's name to? (Gen. 32:28)

Answers: 1. Shield, 2. 100 years old, 3. Forty days, 4. 27, 5. Israel

My Child's Heart Series #2

Fun Time #9

God tells us that the greatest commandment is love. If we love others, we will automatically do all of the other commandments.

Fill in the missing words that tell us what love is in 1 Corinthians 13:4-8 (CEV).

Love is k_____d and p_____t, never j_____s, boastful, p_____d, or rude. Love isn't s_____h or quick tempered. It doesn't keep a record of w_____s that others do. L____e rejoices in the t_____h, but not in evil. Love is always supportive, loyal, h_____l, and t_____g.

Chapter 10
It's Hard to Obey God's Rules

God knew that it wasn't going to be easy to follow all of His commandments. So He sent Jesus Christ down to earth to live just like you and me. Jesus was born of a virgin mother. He had siblings just like some of you. He had to deal with His parents telling Him what to do as well. So Jesus knows how you feel when your parents are always getting on you for doing wrong or telling you to do something in the middle of your favorite game. So He can help you be obedient to your parents even when you don't want to.

Right after Jesus was baptized, He went into the wilderness for forty days. There, He was tempted by Satan. Wow, even Jesus knows what it is like to be offered great things by Satan. The Bible tells us in Mark 1:13 that the angels ministered to Jesus to help Him not give into Satan's temptations. Satan can tell us some really good lies to cause us to do bad things. But Jesus did not give into Satan's temptations so He can help us to not give in.

Jesus came down to earth to be with us and to show us God's love. This was a very important job. As children, you have a very important job and that is to learn about Jesus and to go to school. Sometimes we forget about our important jobs because we are involved in so many sports and other activities, but Jesus can help us with this too. He had so much to do during His short time on earth that He had to focus on those things that were important. He didn't allow other things to get in His way. So Jesus can help us focus on the right things.

It is hard to follow God's rules, but with Jesus' help we can be successful. When we make Jesus our friend, He will walk along with us and help us to do what is right. I am sure you have many friends. Good friends will help you do what is right. Jesus is a very good friend! He helps me all of the time. When we make Jesus our friend, He will make it easier for us to follow God's rules.

It's Hard to Obey God's Rules

Think About It

Parent/Teacher:

Share how being close to God has helped you keep from sinning.

Write ten words that describe what you are like kind, gentle, grumpy, or angry. Share whether these are godly characteristics.

Children:

Who can help you obey God's rules?

Write ten words that describe what you are like kind, gentle, grumpy or angry. Share whether these are godly characteristics.

Key Verse

For to us a child is born, to us a son is given, and the government will be on his shoulders. And he will be called Wonderful Counselor, Mighty God, Everlasting Father, Prince of Peace.

(Isa. 9:6, NIV)

Prayer Time

Dear God, I know it will be hard to obey your rules, but help me to do it. Thank you for giving me the Holy Spirit to help me. Amen.

My Child's Heart Series #2

BIBLE QUIZ #10

Challenge your parents or sibling and see who can answer the most questions below correctly. Don't look at the answers below until you have finished.

1. Abel attended sheep, what did Cain do? (Gen. 4:2)
    a. Fished
    b. Farmed
    c. Raised cows

2. What man was asked to sacrifice his son? (Gen. 22:1-2)
    a. Noah
    b. Abraham
    c. Isaac

3. Who had twelve sons? (Gen. 35:22)
    a. John
    b. Isaac
    c. Jacob

4. Which of Jesus' disciples walked on water? (Matt. 14:29)
    a. Peter
    b. Paul
    c. John

5. According to Proverbs, what separates close friends? (Prov. 16:28)
    a. Money
    b. Gossip
    c. Laziness

Answers: 1. Farmed, 2. Abraham, 3. Jacob, 4. Peter, 5. Gossip

It's Hard to Obey God's Rules

Fun Time #10

Cross out all words that may be considered a sin or something that would be wrong in God's eyes.

(NOTE: Do not cross out the words "sins" and "unrighteous")

BITTERNESS	FOR	QUARRELSOME	WICKEDNESS	JEALOUSY	GOSSIP	CHRIST
HATE	UNFAITHFULNESS	FILTHY TALK	DIED	LYING	IMMORALITY	LAZINESS
FOR	ARGUING	SINS	SLANDER	COVETING	IDOLATRY	LYING
MURDER	ONCE	KILLING	BLASPHEMY	ADULTRY	FOR	SELFISHNESS
STEALING	SLANDER	RAGE	STINGY	ALL,	GREED	THE
RIGHTEOUS	ENVY	ARROGANCE	FOR	PRIDE	GLUTTONY	QUARRELSOME
FOOLISHNESS	THE	COMPLAINING	LUST	UNRIGHTEOUS,	IMPURITY	STEALING
TO	GAMBLING	BRING	RACISM	WICKEDNESS	YOU	WORRY
UNKINDNESS	PRIDE	TO	IDOLATRY	GOD	ANGER	DISOBEDIENCE

What do the remaining words say? Write them in order on the lines below.

_____

_____

_____

1 Peter 3: 18a (NIV)

Chapter 11
Jesus Our Helper

Obeying God's rules would be impossible without the Holy Spirit. Since Jesus is our best friend, when He left to go back to heaven, He didn't want us to be alone. So He gave all of His believers the Holy Spirit. *"Jesus replied, 'If anyone loves me, he will obey my teaching. My Father will love him, and we will come to him and make our home with him. He who does not love me will not obey my teaching. These words you hear are not my own; they belong to the Father who sent me. All this I have spoken while still with you. But the Counselor, the Holy Spirit, whom the Father will send in my name, will teach you all things and will remind you of everything I have said to you'"* (John 14:23-26, NIV).

The Holy Spirit was sent to be our counselor. A counselor is someone who helps us choose what is right. Isn't it awesome to know that Jesus didn't leave us alone? It is good to know that Jesus is living right in our hearts.

Although the Holy Spirit lives within us, we must listen to hear the Holy Spirit. We must choose to obey. You probably have many lights in your house. At nighttime when the lights are off, it is very hard to see where you are going. If you tried to walk around with the lights off, you would probably run into something and possibly hurt yourself. How many of you have hit your toe on the bed because you couldn't see the post? Well, when the Holy Spirit is in us, He guides us through life and prevents us from running into things and getting hurt.

Unfortunately, lights do not come on by themselves. Most lights have an on/off light switch. In order for the light to come on, you have to put the switch in the on position. This is how it is with the Holy Spirit. The Holy Spirit doesn't automatically turn on. You have to listen to Him and surrender your heart to His teaching. You decide whether the Holy Spirit is going to be light to help you do the right thing.

So many times we ignore the Holy Spirit because we are only thinking about ourselves. So when the Holy Spirit (light) is on; a path is lit for you and you know the right thing to do.

When we turn on the Holy Spirit, it will teach our minds how to think like Jesus. It leads us down the right path and helps us make good decisions. The Holy Spirit will also control our emotions. Jackson was playing with his friends outside and a bully came by and started teasing them. He called Jackson and his friend losers. His friend became angry and threw a rock at the bully. Jackson wanted to become angry, but the Holy Spirit helped him control his feelings. Instead of talking mean to the bully, Jackson just held his tongue. When someone attacks us physically or with words, we naturally want to hurt them back. But the Word of God tells us to love our enemies, and this is what the Holy Spirit helps us to do. He will tell us not to pay people back with evil. This is God's job. *"But I tell you to love your enemies and pray for anyone who mistreats you"* (Matt. 5:44, CEV).

David couldn't believe that his brothers, friends, and other Israelites were afraid to fight the Philistines. He thought, *They don't have a wonderful, powerful, trusting God like us. He has always helped me to protect my sheep from wild animals. If He will protect my sheep, surely He will protect me.* So he went to Saul, the king in charge of the army, and told him that he would fight Goliath. Everyone laughed because he was a small young boy. He couldn't even fit into the army uniform. David didn't care about them laughing at him because he knew he could do anything with God's help. So David

Jesus Our Helper

marched out of Saul's tent and headed for Goliath. God gave him the courage to fight his enemy because it was the right thing to do. David was not afraid to do what was right. We should expect God to give us courage to do what is right. All we have to do is pray for it and know that He will give it to us.

God told Moses that He wanted him to lead His people to the Promised Land. Moses didn't feel like he could do this because he didn't speak well. So God told him to take his brother and let him speak if this made him feel better. Wasn't that nice of God to help Moses this way? He could have said, "I don't care about you being afraid to speak to others! Just do what I say"! Our God is a helpful God; He wants to help us to do what is right. So Moses led the people out of Egypt. Well, Moses needed some more help. The Israelites were not happy people. They complained about everything. No matter how much Moses did, they continued to complain about food and being tired. Moses was getting tired of them, but God gave him the patience to deal with them for forty years. You see, all of the Israelites except Moses continued to disobey God, so He punished them. They had to walk around in the wilderness for forty years. And Moses had to stay with them because he was the leader. What a bummer! Moses was being punished for something he didn't do. Has this ever happened to you? What is your attitude when this happens? Moses continued to have joy.

Did You Know?

We face giants like David did with Goliath everyday. David was able to beat Goliath because he trusted in God. He knew God would help him. We beat our giants when we ignore people when they say mean things to us, when we don't go along with those who are doing the wrong thing, and when we don't always think about ourselves first.

Jesus Our Helper

Think About It

Parent/Teacher:

Tell of a time when the Holy Spirit stopped you from doing something wrong.
How do you feel when you do something wrong?

Children:

Has the Holy Spirit ever talked to you?
Do you feel bad when you do something wrong?

Key Verse

I will strengthen you and help you.

(Isa. 41:10b, NIV)

Prayer Time

Jesus, I know the Holy Spirit is living inside me, but it is hard to listen to Him sometimes. I pray that I will listen to the Holy Spirit more. Amen.

My Child's Heart Series #2

Bible Quiz #11

Challenge your parents or sibling and see who can answer the most questions below correctly. Don't look at the answers below until you have finished.

1. Who tasted the fruit first in the Garden of Eden? (Gen. 3:6)

2. What son did Eve say was a replacement for Abel? (Gen. 4:25)

3. What is the third book of the Old Testament?

4. What is the longest book in the New Testament?

5. For God so loved the world that He gave His only begotten Son, that whoever believes in Him shall_____ (John 3:16)

   a. Have fun for the rest of their lives
   b. Live a long and rich life
   c. Not perish but have eternal life

Answers: 1. Eve, 2. Seth, 3. Leviticus, 4. Acts, 5. Not perish but have eternal life.

Jesus Our Helper

Fun Time #11

Unscramble each of the clue words. Copy the letters in the numbered cells to the matching number cells below.

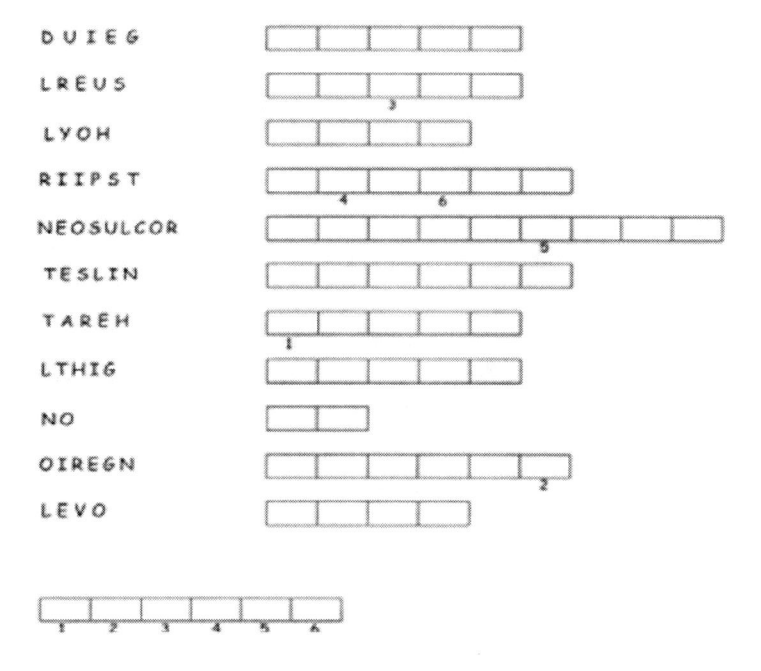

DUIEG

LREUS

LYOH

RIIPST

NEOSULCOR

TESLIN

TAREH

LTHIG

NO

OIREGN

LEVO

Chapter 12
Jesus Our Miracle Worker

The Bible tells us that Jesus performed more than thirty-five miracles during His life. He didn't do this to show off but to show people that He is God. *"Jesus therefore said to Him, 'Unless you people see signs and wonders, you simply will not believe'"* (John 4:48, NASB).

Jesus' first miracle was to turn water into wine. Can you imagine drinking water and all of sudden it is grape juice? Well, this is what happened at a wedding that Jesus attended. It was a custom for everyone to drink wine at the wedding, but the bridegroom had run out. God wanted the wedding to be a success, so He turned water into wine.

Jesus also performed a miracle to feed five thousand people.

"After this, Jesus crossed over to the far side of the Sea of Galilee, also known as the Sea of Tiberias. A huge crowd kept following him wherever he went, because they saw his miraculous signs as he healed the sick. Then Jesus climbed a hill and sat down with his disciples around him. (It was nearly time for the Jewish Passover celebration.) Jesus soon saw a huge crowd of people coming to look for him. Turning to Philip, he asked, 'Where can we buy bread to feed all these people?' He was testing Philip, for he already knew what he was going to do. Philip replied, 'Even if we worked for months, we wouldn't have enough money to feed

My Child's Heart Series #2

them!' Then Andrew, Simon Peter's brother, spoke up. 'There's a young boy here with five barley loaves and two fish. But what good is that with this huge crowd?' 'Tell everyone to sit down,' Jesus said. So they all sat down on the grassy slopes. (The men alone numbered about 5,000.) Then Jesus took the loaves, gave thanks to God, and distributed them to the people. Afterward he did the same with the fish. And they all ate as much as they wanted. After everyone was full, Jesus told his disciples, 'Now gather the leftovers, so that nothing is wasted.' So they picked up the pieces and filled twelve baskets with scraps left by the people who had eaten from the five barley loaves. When the people saw him do this miraculous sign, they exclaimed, 'Surely, he is the Prophet we have been expecting!'

(John 6:1-14, NLT)

Jesus Our Miracle Worker

Jesus can also heal the sick if He chooses to do so. Jesus doesn't heal everyone. He sometimes wants them to be in heaven with Him. *"When this man heard that Jesus had arrived in Galilee from Judea, he went to him and begged him to come and heal his son, who was close to death. The royal official said, 'Sir, come down before my child dies.' Jesus replied, 'You may go. Your son will live.' The man took Jesus at His word and departed. While he was still on the way, his servants met him with the news that his boy was living"* (John 4:47, 49-51, NIV).

Jesus performs the ultimate miracle in all of us who are saved. He turns us from sinners to believers. He cleanses us from all of the dirty stuff and gives us a new life. Jesus said: *"I am the one who raises the dead to life! Everyone who has faith in me will live, even if they die"* (John 11:25, CEV).

If Jesus can perform all of these miracles and more, you should not doubt that He can perform a miracle in your life. He can help you with any problem that you might have. But remember, Jesus doesn't always perform the miracle that we want Him to.

Think About It

Parent/Teacher:

Share with your children something miraculous that Jesus has done in your life or someone else's.

Children:

Do you think Jesus still performs miracles?
What miracle would you like for Him to perform in your life?
Does Jesus promise to do everything that we pray for?
Should we be angry when God doesn't answer our prayers?
Pray and ask God for something you need.

Key Verse

When the people saw him do this miraculous sign, they exclaimed, "Surely, he is the Prophet we have been expecting."
(John 6:14, NLT)

Prayer Time

Jesus, I know that you can still do miracles today. I pray that you will help me to believe in your promises and that you are willing to do miracles in my life. Amen.

Jesus Our Miracle Worker

BIBLE QUIZ #12

Challenge your parents or sibling and see who can answer the most questions below correctly. Don't look at the answers below until you have finished.

1. Laban deceived Jacob into marrying which daughter first? (Gen. 29:18-26)
   a. Rachel
   b. Rebekkah
   c. Leah

2. Who was Jacob's first son? (Gen. 46:8)
   a. Joseph
   b. Reuben
   c. Benjamin

3. The fruit of the spirit is made up of how many traits? (1 Cor. 6:9-10)
   a. fourth
   b. sixth
   c. nine

4. Christ said that He came to call the _____ to repentance. (Matt. 9:13)
   a. Sinners
   b. Good people
   c. Jews

5. First bird Noah sent forth from the ark. (Gen. 8:7)
   a. Dove
   b. Raven
   c. Robin

Answers: 1. Leah, 2. Reuben, 3. Nine, 4. Sinners, 5. Raven

Fun Time #12

```
H E B G D Z M R C B S U H T T
O T C O N O U X P P J P U N N
L J D P E I T X I E Y S E G P
Y N Q V V X V R S N D I S X I
L A M S I L I I W H T U B L Q
J O R I G T C U L A S G E N E
G L V P R K H O P E F U L I Q
M G X E O A F X J T F G I T E
C J P T F Z C B Q Q T T E R G
R E K R O W Y L A E H J V J N
V Q H X T L G G E F S R E O E
X E A R E O N G I T E R F A T
X M D J Y F R P R B L B N A S
E C D N X J W U Z W M W G T I
B U L O Y A L U P G V Q D U L
```

BELIEVE	HOPEFUL	LOVE	PRAY
FORGIVE	JESUS	LOYAL	SICK
HEAL	LISTEN	MIRACLE	SPIRIT
HOLY	LIVING	PATIENT	WORKER

Chapter 13
Jesus Our Best Friend

Jesus wants to do more than perform miracles. He wants to help us when we have a problem. He wants to be our special friend. Friends are the ones you go to for advice; they pray for you and just help you whenever they can. They are always there when you need them. This is what Jesus wants to be for all of us.

Jordan was so excited about starting school. This year she began Kindergarten. She dreamed of this day for so many years. She knew this meant that she was a big girl. Her mom was somewhat worried about this important day because Jordan had to catch the school bus all by herself. No parents were allowed to ride on the bus. So she put Jordan on the bus and told her to remember that God is always with her to guide her. Jordan had a great first day. She loaded the bus to head home. As Jordan passed the many stops, they all looked like her stop. She couldn't remember which one was hers so she got off at the next stop. After walking a little ways, she realized that she had made a mistake. None of the houses looked familiar and she didn't see her mom. Her mom told her she would be waiting at her stop and she forgot about that. Jordan sat down on the curb and began to cry because she was lost. As she began to cry, she remembered what her mother told her. She prayed and asked God to guide her. She asked Him to help her find her way home. As she waited for God to answer, she heard her mother calling her name. She was so glad to see her mother that she jumped up and began to run. She hugged her mother tightly and didn't want to let go. Jordan immediately thanked God for helping her mother find her. She thought God would lead her to her home but He led her mother to her. She thanked her mom for telling her that God is always with her.

Jesus is always with us. It doesn't matter what you are going through; God will always help you.

Kathy had been sick for months with cancer. She told her family members to pray for her. Everybody in the church was praying, even her daughter Nicole. Nicole's mom told her that God had the power to heal but only if it was His will. She told Nicole that people die, even parents, but God is always with us. He will help us through any situation. Nicole didn't understand this *will* thing, but she did understand healing because her mom told her stories about how God healed people in the Bible.

Because of all of the prayers, Nicole just knew her mother would get better. When her mom died, Nicole couldn't understand why God would allow her mother to die. She became angry with God. She told God that she was mad because He had healed all

Jesus Our Best Friend

those people in the Bible, so why not her mother? Nicole couldn't understand why it wasn't God's will to heal her mother. She was a good person and loved Him. She always helped in the church, prayed, and studied the Bible. This didn't make any sense to her.

Nicole's dad could see that she was angry and didn't want to go to church. He told Nicole that her mom had served God well, and He wanted her in heaven with Him. Although he will miss his wife, he knew that God would always be there for him. He told Nicole that God would comfort him when he misses his wife, will help control his emotions when he wants to get angry, and help give him peace about the death. Her father told her, "Jesus didn't come into our hearts to make us worry, sick or sad, He came to give us peace and joy." He opened his Bible and read, *"GOD makes his people strong. GOD gives his people peace* (Ps. 29:11, TM)." He told Nicole to continue to read her Bible and God would comfort her as well.

Nicole trusted her dad, so she read her Bible every day. She read about how God helped David when he lost his son, how He helped Joseph after his brothers sold him into slavery, and how He helped Moses confront Pharaoh. Nicole noticed that after a couple of weeks, she felt better about her mother's death. She stilled missed her mother, but she was not sad all of the time. She thought, *Reading God's Word does work.* So she continued to talk to God and read His Word.

Jesus is the best friend that anyone can have because He knows what we are going through. He has experienced most of the bad things that we have experienced. Jesus was sad when He had to die on the cross, so He knows what it is like to be sad. He was angry when people did bad things in the temple, so He can help you not to be angry. He was hurt on the cross, so He knows what it is like to be in pain. He was sad when the Jews rejected Him and called Him names, so He knows how you feel when kids tease you. He was disappointed when people would not listen to Him and come to Christ, so He understands when your parents do not listen to you or believe you.

So when you are sad, angry, confused or hurt, turn to Jesus. Ask Him to help you feel better. Remember He is your friend!

Think About It

Parent/Teacher:

Is Jesus your friend? Do you take your problems to Him? Share how reading the Bible and going to church has helped you in life.

Children:

Is Jesus your friend? Do you take your problems to Him? How does it make you feel to know that Jesus is always with you?

If your parents aren't around, who can you ask to help you?

Key Verse

But you know the Spirit, who is with you and will keep on living in you.

(John 14:17c, CEV)

Prayer Time

Jesus, thank you for being with me always. Help me to call on you when I need help. Amen.

Jesus Our Best Friend

Bible Quiz #13

Challenge your parents or sibling and see who can answer the most questions below correctly. Don't look at the answers below until you have finished.

1. First person to build an altar unto the Lord. (Gen. 8:20)
   a. Abraham
   b. Noah
   c. Joseph

2. Who was David's dad? (1 Sam. 17:12)
   a. Saul
   b. Jesse
   c. Abraham

3. It was because of David's _____ that God delivered Goliath into his hand. (1 Sam. 17:37, 45-47)
   a. Good shepherding
   b. Obedience
   c. Faith

4. Where did the rock hit Goliath that killed him? (1 Sam. 17:49)
   a. Forehead
   b. Back
   c. Stomach

5. Before David became King, he was a _____. (1 Sam. 16:11-13)
   a. Land tiller
   b. Farmer
   c. Shepherd

Answers: 1. Noah, 2. Jesse, 3. Faith, 4. Forehead, 5. Shepherd

Fun Time #13

Test your parents to see who can match the most children with their dads.

David	Terah
Joseph	Lamech
Jacob	Adam
Seth	Abraham
Ishmael	Jacob
Abraham	Isaac
Solomon	Jesse
Noah	David

Chapter 14
Take a Look at Your Friends

Although Jesus is the best friend that we can have, we still need friends here on earth. We need friends because it's no fun going to the mall and movies by ourselves. We need someone other than God to talk to about our problems. This is where friends come in. Friends are great. I love talking to my friends. God wants us to have friends other than Jesus. But He also warns us about picking the wrong friends.

> Do not be misled: "Bad company corrupts good character."
> (1 Cor. 15:33, NIV)

> Stay away from a foolish man, for you will not find knowledge on his lips.
> (Prov. 14:7, NIV)

He warns us about our friends because He knows that friend's habits and words will rub off on us. So make sure you select friends who have Christ-like behavior. Some people may say they are Christians, but you have to look at how they act. Do they act like Christ? Solomon was the wisest person alive. He followed God and did so many awesome things for God. But Solomon married the wrong wife, and she caused him to worship idols. The Bible tells

My Child's Heart Series #2

us that worshipping idols is a sin. Solomon knew this was a sin, but he did it anyway because he wanted his wife to like him. The Bible tells us that bad company will corrupt us.

Do not pick friends based on...

How they look
How well they dress
How cool they are
How popular they are
The sports they play
How much money their parents have
The cool things they have

Pick friends based on...

Their godliness
    They put God first in their lives
    They try to get you to do the right thing
    They obey their teachers and parents

Take a Look at Your Friends

Their love for others
    They do not tell others' secrets
    They share
    They do not make fun of others

Their gentleness/kindness/goodness
    They are kind to others
    They talk nicely to others
    They help others

Their joyfulness
    They are happy when good things happen to you
    They get excited when you win
    They do not complain all of the time

Their patience
    They wait on God to answer their prayers
    They allow others to be first
    They allow those who cannot play well to be on their team

Their faithfulness
    They tell you when you do something wrong in love
    They obey God's commands
    They are your friend even when you hurt them

It matters who your friends are. True friends are those who encourage you to do right. They should want the best for you. Samson thought Delilah was his friend so he told her that his strength comes from his long hair. Delilah told this secret to the Philistines for money. The Philistines captured him and cut his hair and blinded him. This happened to Samson because he did not choose his wife wisely. Remember to choose your Christians friends wisely, because not all who say they are Christians really are.

Your best friends should be those who are trying to follow God. This does not mean that you are not to be kind and play with those who are not Christians. God tells us to love everybody. In fact, we are to share Jesus with those who do not know Him. Many of your friends are wandering around lost. They don't know God because no one has told them that Jesus loves them. Make sure you share Jesus with all of your friends.

Take a Look at Your Friends

THINK ABOUT IT

Parent/Teacher:

> Share if you have strong Christian friends. How do they help you to follow God?
> Share how a friend led you to sin.

Children:

> Are all people who say they are Christians really Christians?
> Make a list of your friends. Next to each of their names write down if they help you to sin or do the right thing.
> Pray for those who help you to do the wrong thing and ask God to help them.

Key Verse

> Don't fool yourselves. Bad friends will destroy you.
> (1 Cor. 15:33 CEV)

Prayer Time

> *God, I know that it important to choose good friends. Help me to choose godly friends. Help me to be a godly friend. Amen.*

BIBLE QUIZ #14

Challenge your parents or sibling and see who can answer the most questions below correctly. Don't look at the answers below until you have finished.

1. Who was David's best friend? (1 Sam. 20:17)
   a. Saul
   b. Jonathan
   c. Joseph

2. What was Abraham's first wife's name?(Gen. 11:29)
   a. Sarai
   b. Lilah
   c. Rachel

3. How old was Abraham when Isaac was born? (Gen. 21:5)
   a. 70
   b. 100
   c. 250

4. Who is Abraham's Nephew? (Gen. 12:5)
   a. Lot
   b. Reuben
   c. Levi

5. What is Moses' sister's name? (Num. 26:59)
   a. Rachel
   b. Miriam
   c. Leah

Answers: 1. Jonathan, 2. Sarai, 3. 100, 4. Lot, 5. Miriam

Take a Look at Your Friends

Fun Time #14

Search for the words that will help you to see who not to look for in a friend.

```
O C W A L L P R U C Z G J M B
H A N O P I I P D N E Y L O L
C S O J S S S E R D K O Y N A
O K I S L U G Z L J O I F E E
S T O F J X N G W C N J N Y T
Y G A O L P Y W C I X Z E D S
B E D E V E Y G V E Z J E I Y
C G U A H N S O C R R F C G Q
O S S T A C A W L B C O V S V
C V W F V K S D N U C N D Z U
A I P P Q L T R K N H V B M U
J K Q W S E R L M U E V G A B
Q W K U K B O S N E A K Y P V
L U F T C E P S E R S I D F V
X M E A N L S B R T B A J X E
```

CHEAT
COOL
DISRESPECTFUL
DRESS
GOSSIP
LIE
LOOKS

MEAN
MONEY
SELFISH
SNEAKY
SPORTS
STEAL
UNKIND

Chapter 15
Getting to Know Jesus

It is very hard to be friends with someone you don't know. Everybody likes friends, and Jesus is the best. When we don't know Jesus, it is very hard for us to be His friend. He knows all about us, and we have to get to know Him so that we can be the kind of friend to Him that He wants us to be. When you are trying to get to know someone, you normally ask them all sorts of questions. You may ask them, where do you live, who are your parents, what do you like to do, what is your favorite color, what is your telephone number, and so on. In this chapter we are going to learn a little bit about Jesus. Read your Bible to learn more about Jesus.

Jesus Is God

"For to us a child is born, to us a son is given, and the government will be on his shoulders. And he will be called... Mighty God" (Isa. 9:6, NIV). Jesus is the Son of God (Mark 1). Jesus is one of the persons of God (God, Son, Holy Spirit). He is one of the Trinity.

Jesus Became Human Like You and Me

"'The virgin will be with child and will give birth to a son, and they will call him Immanuel'—which means, 'God with us'" (Matt. 1:23, NIV). Jesus is completely God and completely human.

Jesus lived on earth about 2000 years ago. He died at the age of thirty-three. At this age, He had completed everything that God wanted Him to do, so He went back to heaven.

Jesus Is Christ

"And Jacob the father of Joseph, the husband of Mary, of whom was born Jesus, who is called Christ" (Matt. 1:16, NIV). The name Christ means Messiah. Messiah means the anointed one, the one sent by God to save the world. Jesus is the good news for you and me.

Jesus Is Our Light

A light is used to show us how to get around in the dark. "And the light shines in the darkness, and the darkness did not comprehend it" (John 1:5, NASB). Jesus came to show us what is right and wrong. Lights are not needed when the sun is shining, only when it is dark. Well, this world is dark because Satan controls a lot of us. He causes us to do things that are bad. That is why we need Jesus to show us what is right.

Getting to Know Jesus

Jesus Is Savior

Jesus is our Savior. *"Salvation is found in no one else, for there is no other name under heaven given to men by which we must be saved"* (Acts 4:12, NIV). We cannot be saved by going to church, doing good things, or trusting in anybody other than Jesus. Salvation comes only from Jesus. Jesus died on the cross because He loves me and you. Because of His death, we can have a relationship with God.

Who is your best friend? I know who wants to be your best friend. And that is Jesus Christ. He is the best friend anybody can have. He loves us more than anyone else. He came down to earth to get to know us better. Now it is time for you to get to know Him.

Read your Bible every day so you can get to know Jesus. When you do this, He will become your best friend. He wants to be the person you come to when you are hurt. The person you tell all of your secrets. The person you come to for advice and more. The great thing about Jesus is that He will never stop being your friend, even when you make a mistake or hurt Him. Doesn't this sound like a wonderful friend?

When you get to know Jesus, you will realize that He is awesome. No one can love you like Jesus. Jesus is our true friend and there is no one like Him.

Think About It

Parent/Teacher:

> Share how Jesus is your friend.
> What type of things do you share with Jesus?

Children:

> Discuss what you have learned.
> What kind of things can you share with Jesus?
> What can you do to help Jesus become your best friend?

Key Verse

> You are my friends if you do what I command.
> (John 15:14, NIV)

Prayer Time

> *Dear Jesus, thank you for wanting to be my friend. Help me to obey you so I can be your friend. Amen.*

Getting to Know Jesus

Bible Quiz #15

Challenge your parents or sibling and see who can answer the most questions below correctly. Don't look at the answers below until you have finished.

1. Where did Moses first encounter the Lord? (Ex. 3:4)

2. What did Moses hold out over the Red Sea when God parted it? (Ex. 14: 21)
   a. Staff
   b. His Hand
   c. His Sword

3. How old was Moses when he died? (Deut. 34:7)

4. Name Noah's three sons? (Gen. 5:32)

5. Who was the first person to kill someone? (Gen. 4:8)

Answers: 1. The burning bush, 2. Hand, 3. 120, 4. Ham, Shem and Japeth, 5. Cain

My Child's Heart Series #2

Fun Time #15

Set a timer for one minute. Challenge your parents to see who can write the most names that describe Jesus. One has been done for you.

Healer
_____
_____
_____
_____
_____
_____
_____
_____
_____
_____
_____
_____
_____
_____
_____
_____

Chapter 16

What Happens When I Don't Know Jesus?

After leaving Egypt, God spoke to Moses and told him that he must go and rescue His people. Moses didn't feel like he could do this, but God promised that He would help him. God gave Moses the courage to be obedient. Moses did what God told him to do because he had faith in God. Faith means that you believe in God and trust Him. It is obeying God. When we know God and trust Him, it is easier for us to do what He says.

Would you trust a person you just met? If a stranger told you to get into his car, would you? I hope you would not trust a stranger. Well, let's see what happens when someone does not know or trust God.

Although Moses was afraid, he went and told Pharaoh to let God's people go. But Pharaoh didn't know God, so he ignored Moses. God had Moses perform many miracles to convince Pharaoh to let His people go. Moses turned the Nile River into blood. He caused a large number of locusts and frogs to cover the land and the Egyptian's houses. Can you imagine frogs running all through your house and jumping in your food? That would be gross! He had locusts and other insects come and annoy the Egyptians.

My Child's Heart Series #2

Did You Know?

All insects must have three body parts—a head, thorax, and abdomen; six jointed legs; two antennas to sense the world around them; and an exoskeleton (outside skeleton). The most common groups of insects are the beetles, butterflies and moths, ants, bees, wasps, flies, grasshoppers and crickets, and true bugs.

Well Pharaoh was still stubborn even after this, so God put painful sores on the Egyptian's bodies that would not heal. It became dark for three days and nights. They couldn't see to do anything. Finally, all of the first born Egyptian son's and cattle died throughout the land.

What Happens When I Don't Know Jesus?

Wow! God was not happy with Pharaoh. Pharaoh couldn't do what God wanted because he didn't believe in God. Pharaoh believed in another god. God expects us to believe only in Him. When we believe in God, we will do what He says. God will punish us when we don't do what He says. Remember, God warned Pharaoh first. He gave him the chance to do what is right many times. After he continued to do what was wrong, God had to punish him to get him to do right. God loves us very much and wants us to be blessed, but He knows that without discipline, we will continue to do bad things. That is why He tells our parents to punish us when we do wrong.

> Young people are prone to foolishness and fads; the cure comes through tough-minded discipline.
> (Prov. 22:15, TM)

When we know God, we will listen to His Word and the Holy Spirit living inside us. Since God made us, He knows everything about us. He knows what we like and don't like. He knows how many hairs we have on our heads. I bet your best friend doesn't know that! He knows what makes us happy or sad and what our favorite foods and drinks are. He knows everything about us! What do you know about Him? God wants to be our best friend. Just because we cannot see God, doesn't mean He cannot be our friend. Many people have friends in other countries that they cannot see. They cannot see each other, but they talk on the phone or send e-mails. Although we cannot see God, we can talk to Him through prayer, and He talks to us through the Bible. Get to know God by reading your Bible.

My Child's Heart Series #2

THINK ABOUT IT

Parent/Teacher:

Read with your children the verses below to see why God gave us the Bible. I have given you a hint for each Bible verse. Fill in the blanks after you have read the Bible verses.

To know _____ (Ps. 100:3)
To know His word is the _____ (John 17:17b)
To know how to _____ (Prov. 8:33a)
To know He is the one and only _____ (Jer. 10:10a)
To learn about people from the _____ (Rom. 15:4a)
To understand we are _____ (Rom. 3:23)
To know that Jesus is _____ (1 John 5:5)
To show us we need a _____ (Acts 4:12)

Who is your best friend here on earth?
Do you trust what your friend tells you?

Children:

Discuss what you learned.
Who is your best friend here on earth?
Do you trust what your friend tells you?

Key Verse

Come near to God and he will come near to you.
(James 4:8, NIV)

Prayer Time

God, I want to know you. Please help me to spend quality time with you. Amen.

What Happens When I Don't Know Jesus?

Bible Quiz #16

Challenge your parents or sibling and see who can answer the most questions below correctly. Don't look at the answers below until you have finished.

1. Who was the first person to go to heaven without dying? (Gen. 5:24)
   a. Enoch
   b. Elijah
   c. Moses

2. Goliath was a _____ . (1 Sam. 17:4)
   a. Philistines
   b. Jebusites
   c. Egyptians

3. Why did David fight against Goliath? (1 Sam. 17:23-24, 32-37)
   a. He was a mighty warrior
   b. All of the Israelites were afraid to fight Goliath
   c. He thought it would be fun

4. Who wants to have a relationship with you?_____

5. Who broke the relationship with God? (Gen. 3:22-24)
   a. Seth
   b. Noah
   c. Adam and Eve

Answers: 1. Enoch, 2. Philistines, 3. All of the Israelites were afraid, 4. Jesus, 5. Adam and Eve

Fun Time #16

Across

1. Your _____ have authority over you.
4. He created everything.
5. To tell God that what you have done is wrong.
7. The only way to God (hint: Begins with a "s").
8. We are all _____.
9. Not doing what God tells us to do.

Down

2. God's _____ are to protect us.
3. We are never too _____ to be saved.
5. _____ friends help you to be obedient.
6. _____ in the Lord Jesus and you will be saved.

Chapter 17
Jesus Our Everything

When you meet someone, the first thing you do is share your name. Did you know that some names have special meaning? My name is Kathy, which is from the Greek language and it means *pure*. If you have the name Sarah, it means *princess*. Many of us have three names (first, middle, and last). Jesus has many names in the Bible. In fact, He has more than 700 names and titles. God really wants us to understand who Jesus is, so He had people call Him many names and titles. By knowing all His names, we will get know to Him better.

Some people are given other names besides their birth name. You probably do not call your mother or father by their first names. It is disrespectful to call them by their first names. You probably don't call your grandmother or grandfather by their first names either. In life we will get different titles, and this is the same for Jesus. Throughout His life, His roles and titles changed. When we know who Jesus is, we can better understand how He can help us through our day-to-day challenges. Jesus is more than qualified to be God and to help us with anything!

I wonder how Jesus got His name. An angel told Joseph to name Him, Jesus. "*But after he had considered this, an angel of the Lord appeared to him in a dream and said, 'Joseph son of David, do not be afraid to take Mary home as your wife, because what is conceived in her is from the Holy Spirit. She will give birth to a son, and you are to give him the name Jesus, because he will save his people from their sins'"* (Matt. 1:20-21, NIV).

Names and Titles for Jesus

Advocate: A person who fights for us and stands by us. Jesus will help us fight against Satan and unkind people at school when we ask for help and pray to Him.

> My dear children, I write this to you so that you will not sin. But if anybody does sin, we have one who speaks to the Father in our defense—Jesus Christ, the Righteous One.
>
> (1 John 2:1, NIV)

Jesus Our Everything

Bread of life: If we do not eat food and drink water, we will die. When we do not make Jesus our Lord and Savior, we will die. Jesus is like our food. We need to read His Word every day so we will live a life that is pleasing to God. Jesus is all we need!

> He who comes to me will never go hungry, and he who believes in me will never be thirsty.
> (John 6:35, NIV)

Creator: Jesus made everything. He was here from the beginning.

> For by him all things were created: things in heaven and on earth, visible and invisible, whether thrones or powers or rulers or authorities; all things were created by him and for him.
> (Col. 1:16, NIV)

Friend: When Jesus is our friend, He helps us to deal with unkind people, He encourages us to do well and hang in there, and He gives us joy when we are sad

> You are my friends if you do what I command.
> (John 15:14, NIV)

Good Shepherd: A shepherd is someone who leads others. Jesus is our Shepherd and we are the sheep. If we follow Him and His Words, we will not get lost and sin.

> I am the good shepherd. The good shepherd lays down his life for the sheep.
> (John 10:11, NIV)

Master and Lord: Jesus is our ruler and sets all the laws for us. We must do what He says as Lord.

> You call me "Teacher" and "Lord," and rightly so, for that is what I am.
> (John 13:13, NIV)

Mediator: Jesus came down to earth to show us God. He went back to heaven so we can talk to God through Him.

> For there is one God and one mediator between God and men, the man Christ Jesus.
> (1 Tim. 2:5, NIV)

Immanuel: Immanuel means God is with us. God is with us no matter what is going on and no matter where we are.

> The virgin will be with child and will give birth to a son, and they will call him Immanuel—which means, God with us.
> (Matt. 1:23, NIV)

Messiah: Messiah means the anointed One who will deliver Israel. Jesus can deliver us from sin as well.

> The first thing Andrew did was to find his brother Simon and tell him, "We have found the Messiah" (that is, the Christ).
> (John 1:41, NIV)

Prince of Peace: Jesus will bring everlasting peace to us. We do not have to be worried about anything but take all of our worries to Jesus, and He will give us peace.

> Therefore, since we have been justified through faith, we have peace with God through our Lord Jesus Christ.
> (Rom. 5:1, NIV)

Redeemer: One who frees or delivers another from difficulty, danger, or bondage, usually by the payment of a ransom price. Jesus frees us from being sad, lonely, angry, and selfish. He died on the cross so we can stop sinning and feeling bad.

> For even the Son of Man did not come to be served, but to serve, and to give his life as a ransom for many.
> (Mark 10:45, NIV)

Jesus Our Everything

The Rock: A rock is something that is strong and stable. It does not change. When we depend on Jesus, He will give us strength. We will not fall or give into sin.

> The LORD lives! Praise be to my Rock! Exalted be God, the Rock, my Savior!
>
> (2 Sam. 22:47, NIV)

The Word: Jesus is called the Word because Jesus was sent to tell us about God. Jesus Christ is the message in the Bible.

> In the beginning was the Word, and the Word was with God, and the Word was God.
>
> (John 1:1, NIV)

Did You Know?

The Old Testament Bible was first written in the Hebrew language. In this language Jesus had many names as well. In fact, the Hebrew name for Jesus is *Yeshua*. So let's learn some of Jesus' names and titles in Hebrew.

JEHOVAH means *Lord* in English

JEHOVAH-JIREH means *the Lord will provide*. Jesus will take care of our needs if we ask.

JEHOVAH-ROPHE means *the Lord who heals*. Jesus has the power to heal so don't be afraid to pray for healing.

JEHOVAH-NISS means *God does our battles for us*. Jesus will help us fight against a bad habit and our enemy.

JEHOVAH-M'KADDESH means *the Lord who sanctifies*. Jesus has the power to remove all of our sins, no matter what they are.

JEHOVAH-SHALOM means *the Lord of Peace*. Jesus can give us peace in a difficult situation.

JEHOVAH-ROHI means *the Lord is our shepherd.* Jesus wants to show us what is best for us. We need to follow Him.

It is important for us to know and remember these names so we will know God and the power of God. When we pray, it is good to use these names of God to show Him that we know all about Him.

Jesus Our Everything

Think About It

Parent/Teacher:

> Share with your children the meaning of their names.
> Share how you can use the names and titles of Jesus to help you in life.
> Pick one name or title of Jesus and tell how you can use that to help with something that is going on in your life.

Children:

> Share what you have learned.
> Pick one name or title of Jesus and tell how you can use it to help with something that is going on in your life.

Key Verse

> You call me "Teacher" and "Lord," and rightly so, for that is what I am.
>
> (John 13:13, NIV)

Prayer Time

> *Dear God, thank you for giving Jesus all of His wonderful names. Help me to remember His names so I can use them when I need them. Amen.*

My Child's Heart Series #2

BIBLE QUIZ #17

Challenge your parents or sibling and see who can answer the most questions below correctly. Don't look at the answers below until you have finished.

1. Who made it possible for us to have a relationship with God again? (John 14:6a)
   a. Jesus
   b. Adam
   c. Abraham

2. What must you do when you sin? (Luke 15:7)

3. What is Ruth's mother in law's name? (Ruth 1:1-5)
   a. Mary
   b. Naomi
   c. Janah

4. Who wrote the Book of Proverbs? (Prov. 1:1)
   a. David
   b. Solomon
   c. Saul

5. According to Jesus, how many times should a man forgive his brother if he sins against him? (Matt. 18:21-22).

Answers: 1. Jesus, 2. Repent, 3. Naomi, 4. Solomon, 5. 490

Jesus Our Everything

FUN TIME #17

Cross out the letters *x* and *z* to discover how the Holy Spirit will help you.

Buxt the Cozunzselor, the Holzy Spirit, whozm the Fatxher will sendz in my nxame, will tezach you all thinxgs and will remiznd you of everzything I haxve saizd to you. (John 14:26, NIV)

[Inverted text at bottom of page:] But the counselor, the Holy Spirit whom the Father will send in my name will teach you all things and will remind you of everything I have said to you. (John 14:26, niv).

Chapter 18
Jesus Our Heart

Have you ever noticed that you begin to talk and act like your best friend? I noticed the other day that my daughter says, "There you go" and I say that as well. I stopped to figure out where I got that phrase and realized that my best friend says it. Just like we repeat words and behaviors of our family and friends, God expects us to act like Jesus after we are saved.

When we start hanging around Jesus by reading His Word, we will start talking and acting like Him. Jesus put the Holy Spirit in us to make sure that we remember Him. The Holy Spirit only lives in those who are saved. The Holy Spirit reminds us that Jesus is loving, joyful, peaceful, patient, kind, good, faithful, gentle, and self controlled. Now that the Holy Spirit is in us, we can be these things as well. Galatians 5:22-23 tells us, *"God's Spirit makes us loving, happy, peaceful, patient, kind, good, faithful, gentle, and self-controlled. There is no law against behaving in any of these ways"* (CEV).

With the Holy Spirit's help, we can act like Jesus. We can show that wonderful fruit of the Spirit that God put in us. When we live by the fruit of the Spirit, we show God that we love Him. So start living by the fruit of the Spirit.

My Child's Heart Series #2

Fruit of the Spirit

Love

Love cares more for others than for self. Love doesn't always think "me first." Love doesn't keep score of the sins of others.

My command is this: Love each other as I have loved you.
(John 15:12, NIV)

Love is…

1. Letting my brother or sister watch what they want to watch on television.
2. Sharing my things with family and friends.
3. Allowing someone who is not very good to play on my team.
4. Not laughing when someone makes a mistake.
5. Forgiving others when they hurt me.

Jesus Our Heart

Joy

Jesus Christ has given us a spirit of joy. You may know someone who is sick or your friends may mistreat you. These things can make you sad, but Jesus tells us to have joy always.

> If you obey and do right, a light will show you the way and fill you with happiness.
> (Ps. 97:11, CEV)

Joy is…

1. Not pouting when I get in trouble.
2. Smiling even though I don't feel well.
3. Being excited when someone else wins.
4. Not complaining when I have to do something that I don't like.
5. Counting my blessings and not my problems.

Peace

When things are upsetting, confusing, or not going your way, don't worry. Pray and ask God to help you. Give your worries to Him and leave them.

> Peace I leave with you; my peace I give you. I do not give to you as the world gives. Do not let your hearts be troubled and do not be afraid.
> (John 14:27, NIV)

Peace is…

1. Giving all of my worries to God and believing that He will take care of them.
2. Not being afraid to sleep in my room or to tell someone when they are wrong,
3. Working things out with my family and friends in a loving manner and not fighting or arguing.

Patience

Have you ever asked for something and had to wait? Did you do a good job waiting? When we ask for things from our parents and God, we have to wait happily and patiently.

> Therefore, as God's chosen people, holy and dearly loved, clothe yourselves with compassion, kindness, humility, gentleness and patience.
> (Col. 3:12, NIV)

Patience is...

1. Waiting for a slow person to take his or her turn.
2. Waiting for my parents to give me the gift I want.
3. Waiting for my friends to apologize.
4. Waiting for God to answer my prayers.

Gentle/Kind/Good

Do you like it when others are kind to you? What about when they are mean to you? When you are trying to decide what to do or say, think about what you would want others to say and do to you.

> Treat others as you want them to treat you.
> (Matt. 7:12, CEV)

Gentle/Kind/Good is ...

1. Not saying hurtful things to someone even if they have hurt me.
2. Helping others even when I don't feel like it.
3. Sharing even when it is all I have.
4. Including everyone in my game.

Faithful

Faithful means trustworthy, honest, and loyal. We need to be loyal and honest to God, family, friends, and ourselves.

Jesus Our Heart

You will keep your friends if you forgive them, but you will lose your friends if you keep talking about what they did wrong.

(Prov. 17:9, CEV)

Faithfulness is…

1. Trusting what God says in the Bible.
2. Telling a friend or family member when they do something wrong in love.
3. Continuing to love someone even after they have hurt me.

Self-control

Self-control is keeping our feelings and actions under control. Stop and think before you act. Think about the consequences of your actions before you act. Think about whether it will hurt someone or yourself.

A fool gives full vent to his anger; but a wise man keeps himself under control.

(Prov. 29:11, NIV)

Self Control is……

1. Not doing what I feel like doing but what God wants me to do.
2. Not getting angry when I am mistreated.
3. Not throwing a tantrum when I don't get my way.
4. Treating people kindly even when I am angry.

God gave us these fruit because He expects us to use them. God expects even children to have these fruit in their lives. He tells you this in 1 Tim. 4:12, *"Don't let anyone look down on you because you are young, but set an example for the believers in speech, in life, in love, in faith and in purity"* (NIV).

It takes practice for us to get it right. Don't be sad or discouraged if you do not see all of the fruit of the spirit in you. No one is perfect. Pray and ask God to help you develop the missing fruit in your life.

My Child's Heart Series #2

Think About It

Parent/Teacher:

> Share which Fruit of the Spirit comes easily for you.
> Share which Fruit of the Spirit you find most difficult.
> Find scripture in the Bible to help you with the one that is a difficult.

Children:

> Share which Fruit of the Spirit comes easily for you.
> Share which Fruit of the Spirit you find most difficult.
> Find scripture in the Bible to help you with the one that is a difficult.
> How can controlling your feelings help you?

Key Verse

> Don't let anyone look down on you because you are young, but set an example for the believers in speech, in life, in love, in faith and in purity.
>
> (1 Tim. 4:12, NIV)

Prayer Time

> *Dear God, I know all of the fruit of the spirit is in me because I am saved. Please help me to show all of them. Amen.*

Jesus Our Heart

Bible Quiz #18

Challenge your parents or sibling and see who can answer the most questions below correctly. Don't look at the answers below until you have finished.

1. Who was Joseph's mother? (Gen. 30:22-24)

2. Why did Joseph receive a coat of many colors from Israel? (Gen. 37:3)
   a. His father loved him very much
   b. Joseph was cold
   c. He didn't have anyone else to give it too

3. Who bought Joseph from the Ishmaelites? (Gen. 37:36)
   a. Potiphar
   b. Pharaoh
   c. Judah

4. Who was in prison with Joseph? (Gen. 40:2-3)
   a. Joseph's brothers
   b. Jacob
   c. The chief cupbearer and baker

5. What did Joseph do for Pharaoh? (Gen. 41:15-16)
   a. He played the harp for him
   b. He interpreted his dream
   c. He saved Pharaoh

Answers: 1. Rachel, 2. His father loved him very much, 3. Potiphar, 4. The cup bearer and baker, 5. He interpreted his dream

Fun Time #18

Cross out all words that are Fruits of the Spirit.

PATIENT	KIND	TREAT	HAPPY/ JOYFUL	PEACEFUL	GOOD	SELF CONTROLLED
GENTLE	PEACEFUL	FAITHFUL	PATIENT	OTHERS	KIND	PEACEFUL
AS	SELF CONTROLLED	LOVING	GOOD	PATIENT	HAPPY/ JOYFUL	FAITHUFL
GOOD	FAITHFUL	GENTLE	YOU	PATIENT	LOVING	SELF CONTROLLED
KIND	WANT	HAPPY/ JOYFUL	LOVING	THEM	KIND	FAITHFUL
GENTLE	SELF CONTROLLED	TO	HAPPY/ JOYFUL	GOOD	GENTLE	PEACEFUL
TREAT	FAITHFUL	LOVING	KIND	YOU	GENTLE	SELF CONTROLLED

What do the remaining words say? Write them in order on the lines below.

_____

_____

_____

Matthew 7:12

Chapter 19
Jesus Our Guide

With the power of the Holy Spirit, acting like Jesus is not as hard as you think. Do you remember the first time your parents or teacher gave you a book to read? You probably stared at it, wondering what those strange letters on the page were and how anyone could read them. Since you didn't know how to read the words; you just read the pictures. However, in kindergarten or first grade, your parents or teacher shared with you that each letter has its own sound. Now things began to make more sense. Once you learned the sounds, you could read small words. It was still hard for you to read big words. So when you came to the big words, you had to ask your teacher or parents for help.

When it comes to doing the big things that Jesus did, we have to call on the Holy Spirit to help us. Each day we will learn from the Holy Spirit more and more about how to follow Jesus. Each day it will get easier and easier to be like Jesus.

Jesus didn't want us to be alone when He left, so He gave us the Holy Spirit. He wanted us to have someone to help us be like Him. Having the Holy Spirit living inside us is really cool. It is cool because Jesus left us with himself. The Holy Spirit is one of the persons of God. He is part of the Trinity (God, Son, Holy Spirit). Isaiah 11:2 tells us a lot about the Holy Spirit.

My Child's Heart Series #2

> The Spirit of the LORD will rest on him— the Spirit of wisdom and of understanding, the Spirit of counsel and of power, the Spirit of knowledge and of the fear of the LORD.
>
> (Is. 11:2, NIV)

Spirit of Wisdom and Understanding

You cannot get wisdom from your teacher, parents, or friends. Wisdom and understanding comes only from God. Wisdom will help us understand the Bible. It will help us make good choices. It will help us be successful in school and with our friends.

> I guide you in the way of wisdom and lead you along straight paths.
>
> (Prov. 4:11, NIV)

> For the LORD gives wisdom, and from his mouth come knowledge and understanding.
>
> (Prov. 2:6, NIV)

Spirit of Counsel

The Holy Spirit is our counselor. Counselors are people who help us solve problems and make decisions. Every day we should ask the Holy Spirit to help us make good decisions. Nothing is too small for you to ask the Holy Spirit to help with.

> And I will ask the Father, and he will give you another Counselor to be with you forever.
>
> (John 14:16, NIV)

> But the Counselor, the Holy Spirit, whom the Father will send in my name, will teach you all things and will remind you of everything I have said to you.
>
> (John 14:26, NIV)

Spirit of Power

The Holy Spirit is God, so He can do anything you ask if He chooses. The Holy Spirit gives us strength and power to do hard

Jesus Our Guide

things. He gives us strength to confront someone who is mistreating us. He gives us strength to make it through school even when we are tired. He gives us the strength to choose what is right when Satan is tempting us. The power of God is in us!

> He gives strength to the weary and increases the power of the weak.
> (Is. 40:29, NIV)

> Finally, be strong in the Lord and in his mighty power.
> (Eph. 6:10, NIV)

Spirit of Knowledge

This knowledge can only come after we have wisdom and fear of the Lord. God gives knowledge to those with wisdom. Many of us go to school to be smart and to get knowledge. But the true knowledge we should be seeking is knowledge about God. The knowledge that we learn from reading the Bible is far more important than what we learn at school. This doesn't mean that school is not important, because it is. God uses what we learn in school to help us better serve Him.

> I, wisdom, dwell together with prudence; I possess knowledge and discretion.
>
> (Prov. 8:12, NIV)

> The fear of the LORD is the beginning of knowledge, but fools despise wisdom and discipline.
>
> (Prov. 1:7, NIV)

Spirit of the Fear of the Lord

When the Holy Spirit comes to live in us, it causes us to fear the Lord. God doesn't want us to be afraid of Him but to respect and honor Him. He wants us to make Him important and put Him first in our lives. He wants us to know that He is all powerful and can do anything. The best way to show that you fear God is to obey His commandments. When we fear the Lord, He tells us that we will be blessed. I love blessings! How about you?

> Fear the LORD, you his saints, for those who fear him lack nothing.
>
> (Ps. 34:9, NIV)

> He will bless those who fear the LORD— small and great alike.
>
> (Ps. 115:13, NIV)

The Holy Spirit knows what God wants us to do so listen when He speaks. He gives us the power to obey God!

Jesus Our Guide

THINK ABOUT IT

Parent/Teacher:

Share with your children how you continued to make mistakes after you were saved.

Share how you continue to love him or her even when he or she makes mistakes.

Children:

Name an area in your life in which you could use wisdom. (Maybe you need to know how to handle a person who is teasing you, maybe you need help with your math, etc.)

List two things that you would like an answer for from God. Pray and ask God for an answer.

Key Verse

Fear the LORD, you his saints, for those who fear him lack nothing.

(Ps. 34:9, NIV)

Prayer Time

Dear God, thank you for the Holy Spirit that guides me. Help me to fear you Lord so that I may follow your ways. Amen.

My Child's Heart Series #2

Bible Quiz #19

Challenge your parents or sibling and see who can answer the most questions below correctly. Don't look at the answers below until you have finished.

1. How many people were in the ark? (Gen. 7:13)

2. Who told Noah to leave the ark? (Gen. 8:15-16)
    a. Noah himself
    b. God
    c. His wife

3. What did the dove bring back to the ark? (Gen. 8:11)
    a. A Twig
    b. Olive leaf
    c. Grass

4. Why was Noah saved from the flood? (Gen. 6:9)
    a. He was the oldest
    b. He was a righteous man
    c. He knew how to take care of animals

5. She was the mother of all living. (Gen. 3:20)
    a. Eve
    b. Ruth
    c. Sarah

Answers: 1. Eight, 2. God, 3. Olive leaf, 4. He was a righteous man, 5. Eve

Jesus Our Guide

Fun Time #19

How many words can you make from the words below? Compete against your parents or sibling.

HOLY SPIRIT

Chapter 20
Hanging Out with Jesus

Matthew enjoys hanging around his friend Nathan. He likes Nathan because he helps him to do what is right. Matthew also likes to play video games, which Nathan has a lot of. Matthew gets to spend a lot of time with Nathan because he is in his classroom at school and church. They even get to see one another on weekends sometimes. Matthew and Nathan think it is so cool to get to hang around each other as much as they do. But they are always bummed when summer comes because they don't get to see each other as much.

Jesus wants to hang out with us as well. Jesus tells us to abide in Him and He will abide in us. Abide means to spend time with. Just like we find time to spend with our best friends; God expects us to find time for Him. So if we don't find time for God, God will not find time for us. You probably have so much to do every day that it is hard to think about finding time to spend with God. God expects us to spend time with Him every day. I can hear some of you saying that is impossible! Let's take a look at some things that might be stealing time from God.

Television: Watching television is fun, but it doesn't help you grow close to God. In fact, most of the shows on television show you how to act like someone who is not a Christian.

Video Games: I know video games are fun, but sitting down and playing them during the week for hours is a waste of time. This is time you could be reading your Bible.

Telephone: The telephone is a great way to catch up with friends. Be careful about too much telephone time. Talking a lot opens the door for Satan to come in and have you talking badly about others and discussing things that are not godly.

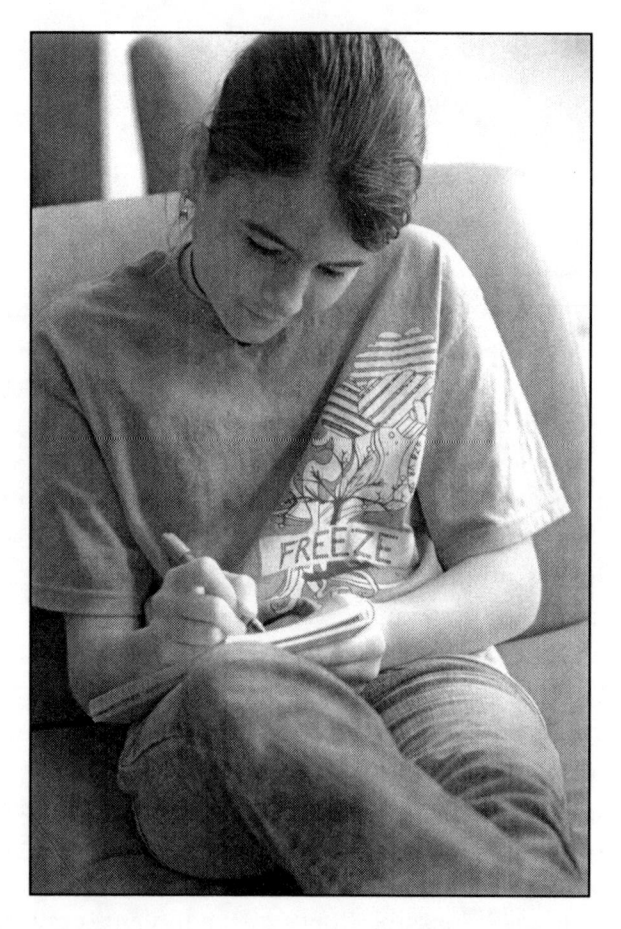

Sports/Activities: Are you running from activity to activity? Do you have very little time to spend at home doing nothing or to do homework or to hang out with your family and God? If this is you, decide what activities you really love and do only those.

Hanging Out with Jesus

Did You Know?

> Pharaoh had a hard heart. When you have a hard heart, you don't do what God says. Have you ever left a piece of bread out on the table overnight? If you did, it was probably hard in the morning. The bread got hard because it didn't have the plastic bag to protect it. When we do not follow God's rules that protect us, our hearts get hard. We begin to sin more and more. To keep your heart soft, you have to read the Bible and obey God's Word.

Sports, clubs, and social events are great but not necessary for your main purpose. God put you on this earth to have a friendship with Him and to tell people about Him. If you are not doing this, you are not pleasing God. When you get to heaven, God is not going to say, "How many touchdowns did you get, how many medals did you get in gymnastics, or how many people thought you were cool?" He will ask, "How many people did you lead to Christ, how many people did you serve or help in your free time?" Focus on the things that are pleasing to God. Put God first!

I know God is competing with television, your friends, after school activities, homework, and the Internet. Each day God gives us twenty-four hours to use as we please. Doesn't He deserve some of this time since He gave it to us? Putting God first in the morning will help you remember Him. Wake up at least fifteen minutes early each morning and read the Bible or a devotional like this one for ten minutes. Then write in your journal for three minutes. Then pray to God the last two minutes. Repeat all of this again before you go to bed. This is not too bad is it? I didn't tell you to give up television, video games, sports, or your friends. I just want you to spend more time with God. He deserves it!

THINK ABOUT IT

Parent/Teacher:

How much time are you spending with God everyday? Are you setting a great example for your children?
Make a commitment to spend your first minutes in the morning and before bed with God. Your children need to see you doing this.
Make sure your children have a Bible or devotional to study every day.

Children:

How much time are you spending with God every day?
Set your alarm fifteen minutes earlier in the morning so you can spend time with God. Remember to go to bed early so you will wake up when your alarm goes off.

Key Verse

Turn my eyes away from worthless things; preserve my life according to your word.

(Ps. 119:37, NIV)

Prayer Time

Dear God, help me to put you first every day. Please forgive me for making other things more important than you. Amen.

Hanging Out with Jesus

Bible Quiz #20

Challenge your parents or sibling and see who can answer the most questions below correctly. Don't look at the answers below until you have finished.

1. Who was the father of Ephraim and Manasseh? (Gen. 48:1)
    a. Jacob
    b. Joseph
    c. Judah

2. Which son found Noah drunk? (Gen. 9:22)
    a. Ham
    b. Japheth
    c. Shem

3. The father of Jonathan (David's best friend). (1 Sam. 19:1)
    a. Solomon
    b. Saul
    c. Levi

4. Eve was tempted in this garden. (Gen. 2:15)
    a. Eden
    b. Gethsemane
    c. Babylon

5. The son born to Sarah when she was old. (Gen. 21:2-3)
    a. Jacob
    b. Cain
    c. Isaac

Answers: 1. Joseph, 2. Ham, 3. Saul, 4. Eden, 5. Isaac

My Child's Heart Series #2

FUN TIME #20

Parent and children, list all of your favorite foods, sports, and games. Tell why these are your favorites.

Chapter 21
Calling Our Best Friend

I love my best friend. I talk to her almost every day. I sometimes talk to her two or three times a day, depending on what's going on. I know that she is there to help me and to listen to me. I am sure you might have a friend like this. If not, I pray that God will bless you with a good friend like mine. Well, my daughter is now in fourth grade, and she is starting to get phone calls from her friends. She and her friends are so excited to talk to each other on the telephone. I noticed that she has written down all of her friend's telephone numbers. She wrote them down so she will be able to call them whenever she wants.

My daughter has numbers for her friends, but how does she call Jesus? What number must she dial to reach Jesus? Jesus is easy to call. You don't need to remember a secret number or have a telephone to reach Him. In fact, you don't even need to be in a special place to call Him. All you need is your mind. You can call Jesus in your head or by using words.

Jesus knows whether He is your best friend based on how often you call Him. If I only called Him once a week, He would know that I like my girlfriend better than Him. Before I tell my husband or girlfriend about my problem, I usually tell Jesus first. He wants us to call Him whenever we want. God is always there to talk to us, unlike our friends. We can talk to God in our house, in our car, in our classroom, or at our soccer game. God is always available and always hears us. He is waiting for us to talk to Him.

Have you ever been talking to someone and realized they are not listening? This happens to me all of the time, and it makes me angry. Well, Jesus is always listening and excited to hear about everything that is going on with us. *"Then you will call upon me and come and pray to me, and I will listen to you"* (Jer. 29:12, NIV).

The most common way to talk to Jesus is through prayer. We get closer to Jesus when we pray. First 1 Peter 5:7 says *"Cast all of your anxiety on him because he cares for you"* (NIV). Don't be afraid to talk to Jesus. He already knows what is going on with us. He just wants us to tell Him on our own. He wants to know that He is our friend.

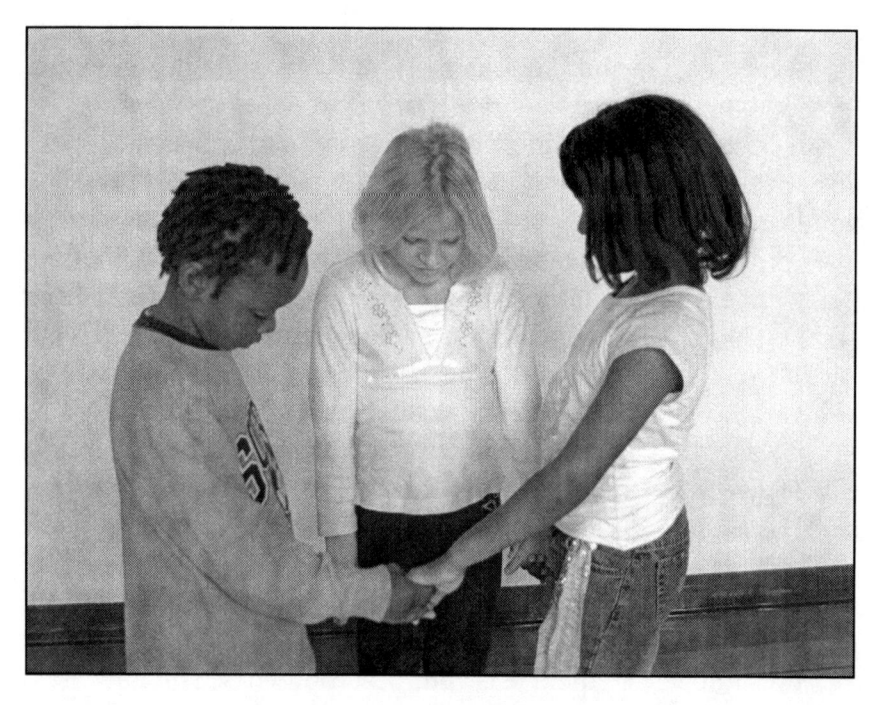

God wants you to pray at all times and for anything. Write down what you pray about in a journal. This will help you see when God answers your prayers. God doesn't always answer our prayers when we want Him to but when it is best for us.

Calling Our Best Friend

Chloe's parents always fought. She would go to her room and pray every night that they would stop. But they continued to fight. She became angry at God because He didn't answer her prayers. She told Him that the Bible says that all good prayers are answered. So she thought God was a liar. She didn't realize that her parents had to want to stop fighting. They had to work on whatever was causing them to fight. You see, her father had a problem with anger. So he would always get mad at her mom. God wanted to answer her prayers, but her father had to realize that being angry caused him to sin. And God was not pleased with this behavior.

Two years later, her father realized that he was not being loving to his wife and children. He decided to go talk to someone who could help him with his anger. He wanted to change, and God helped him. Now, her parents do not fight. Chloe's prayers were answered. It took two years, but it happened.

We have to realize that sometimes we have to be patient with God. God doesn't do things when we want Him to but when He wants to. That is His right as God.

Think About It

Parent/Teacher:

Share with your children how you prayed and God answered. Share a time when you had to wait on God to answer your prayer.
Help your children to start journaling. Get notebooks for you and your children.

1. Encourage them to write down prayers.
2. To list God's blessings.
3. To list when God answered their prayers.
4. To write down how they feel about God.
5. To write down key Bible verses.

Children:

What are some of the things going on in your life that you pray for?
Are there any silly prayers?

Key Verse

The LORD is near to all who call on him, to all who call on him in truth.

(Ps. 145:18, NIV)

Prayer Time

Dear God, thank you for hearing my prayers. Please help me to bring everything to you first. Amen.

Calling Our Best Friend

BIBLE QUIZ #21

Challenge your parents or sibling and see who can answer the most questions below correctly. Don't look at the answers below until you have finished.

1. Who were the twins born to Rebekah? (Gen. 25:21-26)
    a. Cain and Abel
    b. David and Jonathan
    c. Esau and Jacob

2. This son of Isaac was red and hairy. (Gen. 25:25)
    a. Ishmael
    b. Jacob
    c. Esau

3. Jacob's wives had the same father. What was his name? (Gen. 29:10)
    a. Benjamin
    b. Laban
    c. Lamech

4. Who was the oldest of Jacob's wives? (Gen. 29:23-26)
    a. Leah
    b. Rachel
    c. Zilpah

5. Jacob was renamed by God to this name. (Gen. 32:28)
    a. Jacobsen
    b. Jake
    c. Israel

Answers: 1. Esau and Jacob, 2. Esau, 3. Laban, 4. Leah, 5. Israel

My Child's Heart Series #2

Fun Time #21

See how many biblical names you can write in one minute (first names only). Compete against your parents. You have to spell the names correctly.

_____
_____
_____
_____
_____
_____
_____
_____
_____
_____
_____
_____
_____
_____
_____
_____
_____

Chapter 22
Dialing the Right Number

Have you ever tried calling a friend and got the wrong number? It happens to me often. It is important to dial the right number if you want to speak to the person you are calling. When we pray to God, it is important that we are praying for the right things. Dialing up the right number is important, but it is also important to believe that God will answer your prayers when you call Him.

Jesus gave us the Lord's Prayer to teach us how to pray. He doesn't want us to say the prayer word for word. It is just an example of the things we should pray about. Follow our PLANT prayer every day and you will be praying the way Jesus taught us to pray. You will also begin to grow like many plants that are watered and feed each day.

Praise: Tell God how awesome He is and how much you love Him.

You might say, "God you are so wonderful, you created the entire world. I love you because you love me even when I do bad things."

Lead: Ask God to lead you everyday so you will not be tempted by Satan. We need to pray and ask God to give us wisdom, strength and courage to stand firm on His Word and not give into temptations.

You might say, *"Dear God, help me not to get tricked by Satan, myself or anyone else today. Help me to be like Christ today."*

Apologize: Tell God about the wrong things that you have done and ask for forgiveness. Don't just say, "God forgive me of my sins." Tell Him exactly what you did and ask Him to forgive you.

You might say, *"Dear Lord I know it was wrong to scream at my mom, please forgive me and help me to do better."*

Needs: God knows our needs but He wants to hear them from us. This tells Him that we trust Him and know that He controls everything. God will help us with everything. He has unlimited power. Nothing is too big or too small for God.

You might say, *"Dear God, John and Robert are mean to me. Please help them to be kind to me. Help me to be loving and kind to them. Dear God, we have very little food to eat, please provide us our daily food."*

Dialing the Right Number

Thank: Thank God for something every day. Thank God for everything because everything comes from God.

You might say, *"Dear God thank you for my parents, food to eat, a house to live in and my friends. Thank you for sending Jesus Christ to die for my sins."*

Prayer is important in our Christian life. So what do you do when…

- Life doesn't seem fair—**Pray**
- You feel like your parents don't understand you—**Pray**
- Your friends mistreat you—**Pray**
- You don't understand your school work—**Pray**
- Satan is tempting you—**Pray**
- Your parents are fighting—**Pray**
- Things don't seem to be getting better—**Pray**
- A family member or friend is sick—**Pray**
- You started a new school—**Pray**
- You feel lonely—**Pray**
- You are afraid—**Pray**

Think About It

Parent/Teacher:

> Share with your children things that you are thankful for.
> Share with them what you pray about.
> Decide today to pray every day with your children.

Children:

> Share two things that you need help with and pray for them.
> Share two things you are thankful for.

Key Verse

> Be joyful always; pray continually; give thanks in all circumstances, for this is God's will for you in Christ Jesus.
>
> (1 Thess. 5:16-18, NIV).

Prayer Time

> *Dear God, thank you for loving me so and blessing me with many things. Help me to pray only for the important things. Amen.*

Dialing the Right Number

BIBLE QUIZ #22

Challenge your parents or sibling and see who can answer the most questions below correctly. Don't look at the answers below until you have finished.

1. This boy was twelve years old when his parents lost track of him in Jerusalem. (Luke 2:42-45)
   a. David
   b. Jesus
   c. Joshua

2. Who was the boy that God called out to while he was sleeping? (1 Sam. 3:4)
   a. Seth
   b. Samuel
   c. Benjamin

3. The fruit from the tree of knowledge of good and evil that Eve ate from in the garden was a? (Gen. 3:6)
   a. Apple
   b. Pear
   c. Not known

4. What is the strange food that God gave the Israelites in the wilderness? (Gen. 16:31)
   a. Sugar
   b. Leaves
   c. Manna

5. One of the following is known in scripture to have requested a vegetarian diet. (Dan. 1:8)
   a. Moses
   b. Daniel
   c. Peter

Answers: 1. Jesus, 2. Samuel, 3. Not known, 4. Manna, 5. Daniel

My Child's Heart Series #2

Fun Time #22

Unscramble the words in Romans 12:12 to find out what God tells us to do when things are going badly.

tel	rouy	epoh	ekam
uoy	dalg	eB	tneitap
ni	emit	fo	elbuort
dna	reven	pots	gniyarp

Chapter 23
Why Isn't Jesus Answering My Call?

Have you ever prayed for something and thought that God didn't hear you? Sometimes God answers prayers quickly and other times it takes awhile. No matter how long it takes, we have to remember that God hears all prayers.

When God hears our prayers, He stops and thinks if this would be good for us. He considers if this will be good for others. He considers whether He can use our situation to help others learn about Him. I know this is not what you want to hear, but God has to consider everything because we do not. We have to remember that God has our best interest in mind. It is important for us to trust His answers.

God never ignores our prayers. His answer will be either yes, wait awhile, or no. God will tell you His answer through prayer, Bible reading, or deliver it through someone else such as a friend or parent. If, you are not getting an answer to your prayer, you must pray and ask God for the reason. Don't be afraid to ask Him why.

God may wait to answer your prayers or say no because…

It's not good for you

Let's say that you asked for a new bike. Maybe God knows that you are going to ride that bike into the street and get hit by a car. He is preventing this from happening by not giving you the bike.

Don't obey God

God tells us in the Bible that He will bless us when we are obedient. So your prayers may not get answered because you are disobeying your parents. *"We know that God does not hear sinners; but if anyone is God-fearing, and does His will, He hears him"* (John 9:31, NASB).

Don't forgive others

When we don't forgive others for doing bad things to us, God will not forgive us. When we forgive others, God will bless us.

Why Isn't Jesus Answering My Call?

God wants us to trust Him

God sometimes will not stop our big sister from picking on us. He wants us to trust Him and continue to be patient. Romans 12:12 says, *"Let your hope make you glad. Be patient in time of trouble and never stop praying"* (CEV).

God wants others to see Him through us

I know a lady who has cancer, and every time I see her she is smiling. She continues to praise God even though she is hurting every day. I think people can really see God when they talk to her. Some people who do not know God will probably ask her why she is so happy. When they do, she can tell them all about the God who gives her joy during bad times.

Sometimes things really stink, and we want a quick answer. Remember that God knows best. So when you pray and don't get an answer, ask God to give you strength to hang in there until He answers. Continue to pray for understanding. Ask God to show you if you are being disobedient.

Think About It

Parent/Teacher:

> Think of a prayer that God said no to. How did this make you feel?

Children:

> What did you learn?
> What should you do when God takes time to answer your prayer?

Key Verse

> I wait for you, O LORD; you will answer, O Lord my God.
> (Ps. 38:15, NIV)

Prayer Time

> *Dear God, I know you know better than I. Please help me to be patient after I pray. Please help me to pray for the right things and be obedient so you can bless me. Amen.*

Why Isn't Jesus Answering My Call?

Bible Quiz #23

Challenge your parents or sibling and see who can answer the most questions below correctly. Don't look at the answers below until you have finished.

1. Who was born first? (Luke 1)
   a. Jesus
   b. John the Baptist

2. She was the first woman judge of Israel. (Judg. 4:4)
   a. Ruth
   b. Esther
   c. Deborah

3. Who was King David's firstborn son? (1 Chron. 3:1)
   a. Solomon
   b. Absalom
   c. Amnon

4. When putting on the full armor of God, what should be put on first? (Eph. 6:14)
   a. Breastplate of righteousness
   b. The belt of truth
   c. The helmet of salvation?

5. Which brother didn't want to kill Joseph? (Gen. 37:21)
   a. Dan
   b. Reuben
   c. Benjamin

Answers: 1. John the Baptist, 2. Deborah, 3. Amnon, 4. The belt of truth, 5. Reuben

My Child's Heart Series #2

Fun Time #23

Parents and children, on a sheet of paper, draw at least three pictures of a time when you were afraid. Write a sentence for each picture that tells what happened. The sentences should answer these questions.

Was God with me?
Did I remember that God was with me?
What could I have done to not be afraid?

Chapter 24
I Can't Hear Jesus

When we want to hear from Jesus, we sometimes have to listen to our hearts. In the Old Testament, God talked directly to His chosen children, but He doesn't normally talk to us like that today. Today, He uses the Bible and the Holy Spirit to talk to us. So if you don't hear God in your heart, then read the Bible. The Bible is the main way God talks to us. The Bible tells us whether our prayers are pleasing to God, what we should do in a situation, and what we must do to please God. If you are confused about anything, just read your Bible and pray for God to help you understand.

Sam received a remote control car for his birthday. He was so excited to get the car that he ripped open the package and began to play with it. His dad pulled him to the side and began to read the instructions to him, but Sam was not listening. He was too busy thinking about all the fun he could have with his new car. He couldn't wait for his dad to stop talking. His father asked if he understood and heard all of the instructions and Sam, replied that he did. Sam had a great time playing with his remote control car. The next day when Sam's dad was not around, he asked his mom if he could take his car out for a spin. His mom said, "Yes, but don't stay out long because it's raining." Sam had a great time outside

My Child's Heart Series #2

with his car. He played for about thirty minutes and came inside. The next day, when he turned his car on, it wouldn't start. He couldn't figure out what was wrong. His father asked him, "When did you play with the car last?" Sam responded, "Yesterday." His father responded, "You didn't play with it in the rain, did you?" Unfortunately, Sam did not hear his dad when he said, "The car will be destroyed in the rain."

Just like there are instructions on how to work a remote control car, there are instructions for how to live a life that is pleasing to God. God has written all of these instructions in the Bible. *Jesus replied, "That's true, but the people who are really blessed are the ones who hear and obey God's message!" (Luke 11:28, CEV).* Sam is like

I Can't Hear Jesus

some of us Christians; we don't always listen to God's words in the Bible. We make many mistakes and get hurt when we do not do what the Bible tell us. So it is important that we know what the Bibles says so we will not make a mistake like Sam.

The Bible is our food. It helps us grow closer to God. Do you like candy? My children love candy and they have the cavities to prove it. If all you ate was candy, your body would become sick. It would lack the vitamins and minerals that you get from good food like vegetables and fruit. I'm sure you probably complain about eating vegetables like my children. Vegetables don't taste as good as candy but they are important for you to stay healthy and alive. The thoughts that you have about vegetables are probably close to the thoughts you have about the Bible—boring!

The Bible is only boring to those who don't read it a lot. There are some cool stories in the Bible. As you read the Bible, remember that these rules are for us today. Read the Bible like you are reading a text book at school. Read slowly and pay close attention because you will be tested on what you have read. You won't get a written test like your teacher gives you but a life test. Most of you have probably had someone treat you unkindly. If you haven't, you will. The million dollar question is how will you handle it? The Bible tells us to be kind to those who are mean to us and pray for them. If you don't know this, you will fail God's test. Every day God gives us tests to see if we will respond the way the Bible tells us. When we pass the test, God will bless us!

My Child's Heart Series #2

COOL BIBLE STORIES

If you like…	You will love reading about
War and Battles	Israel conquers Canaan (Josh. 10) Gideon (Judg. 6 &7) Battle against Ammonites (1 Chron. 19) David and Goliath (1 Sam. 17, 21:9)
Love story	Ruth and Boaz (Ruth)
Two brothers who hate one another	Jacob and Esau (Gen. 25)
A leader	Moses and Pharaoh (Ex.)
Revenge	Samson's revenge (Judg. 15)
Woman Hero	Esther (Est.)
Adventure	Exodus of the Israelites (Ex.)
Lies	Samson (Judg. 12-16)
Jealous Brothers	Joseph and brothers (Gen. 30-41)
Friendships	David and Jonathan (1 Sam. 20)
Miracles	Lazarus back to life (John 11-12:19)
Super Hero	Jesus (Luke 22-24)
A child who thought his father was crazy	Isaac and Abraham (Gen. 17-18,22)
Happy endings	A hungry little boy (1 Kings 17)
Boys who get into trouble	Meshach,Shadrack,Abednego (Dan. 3)
Romance	Jacob/Rachel (Gen. 29)

Did You Know?

Americans eat more than sixteen pounds of French fries every year. The average person eats the equivalent of ninety-six one-ounce bags of potato chips each year. It takes 10,000 pounds of potatoes to make 3,500 pounds of potato chips. A potato is about 80% water and 20% solid.

I Can't Hear Jesus

Think About It

Parent/Teacher:

Read Joshua 1:8. How often should we read the Bible?
How often do you read the Bible?
a. Every day
b. Once a week
c. Once a month
d. Not very often

How often should you be reading the Bible?
Will you start reading the Bible more?

Children:

How often do you read the Bible?
a. Every day
b. Once a week
c. Once a month
d. Not very often

How often should you be reading the Bible?
Will you start reading the Bible more?

Key Verse

Do not let this Book of the Law depart from your mouth; meditate on it day and night, so that you may be careful to do everything written in it. Then you will be prosperous and successful.
(Josh. 1:8, NIV).

Prayer Time

God, thank you for giving us the Bible. It will help me to know your ways. Amen.

My Child's Heart Series #2

BIBLE QUIZ # 24

Challenge your parents or sibling and see who can answer the most questions below correctly. Don't look at the answers below until you have finished.

1. Who was the wisest man in the world? (1 Kings 3:10-12)

2. What did God tell Abraham to do with Isaac? (Gen. 22:2)

3. Why did Nicodemus visit Jesus secretly at night? (John 3:1-5)
   a. He was seeking the truth.
   b. He wanted to warn Jesus.
   c. He had wanted to give Him some food.

4. Where did Moses receive the Ten Commandments? (Gen. 19:20)
   a. Mount Herod
   b. Mount of Olives
   c. Mount Sinai

5. Who went with Abraham to the foreign land? (Gen. 12:5)
   a. David
   b. Lot
   c. Jacob

Answers: 1. Solomon, 2. Sacrifice him, 3. He was seeking the truth, 4. Mount Sinai, 5. Lot

I Can't Hear Jesus

Fun Time #24

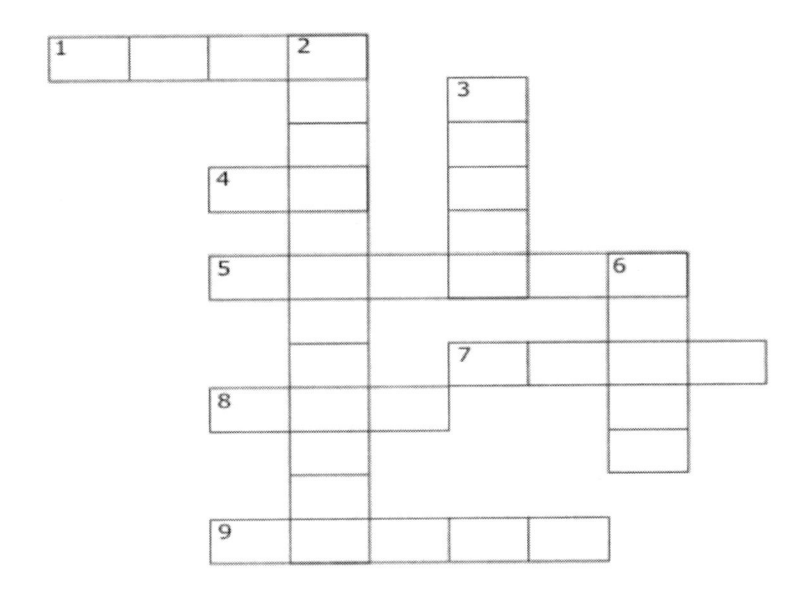

Across

1. God calls the Bible our F_____.
4. Are there any silly prayers?
5. To turn away from sin
7. The Lord's Prayer is to teach us how to _____.
8. Can you pray to God anywhere?
9. Who should we go to first with our problems?

Down

2. Jesus may not answer prayers because of our D_____.
3. God talks to us through this.
6. You should _____ God even when thing are going badly

Chapter 25
Answer Key

Jokes: A Rock hound, A Rock Star, Cocoa Pebbles

Fun Time

Fun Time #1	Fun Time #2
Sat, sail, lion, son, ton, salt, not, lot, as, an, ant, last, list, lost, vast, sit, sin, saliva, lava, tin, tan	Believe that Jesus is Lord and Savior
Fun Time #4	Fun Time #6
Across 1.God 7. Misuse 8. Friends 9. Sports, 10. Vain Down 2. Other, 3. Love, 4. Their 5. Rules, 6. Worshipping	Respect your father and mother, and you will live a long and successful life in the land I am giving you

My Child's Heart Series #2

Fun Time #7

				13
1	5	2	4	12
0	3	4	1	8
4	4	3	1	12
1	3	0	3	7
6	15	9	9	10

Fun Time #8

Across
1. Kill 5. Enemies
6. Complaining 8. God

Down
2. Lie 3. Stealing
4. Rest 7. Obey

Fun Time #9

Love is kind and patient, never jealous, boastful, proud, or rude. Love isn't selfish or quick tempered. It doesn't keep a record of wrongs that others do. Love rejoices in the truth, but not in evil. Love is always supportive, loyal, hopeful, and trusting 1 Corinthians 13:4-8 (CEV).

Fun Time #10

For Christ died for sins once for all, the righteous for the unrighteous to bring you to God

Fun Time #11

Guide, Rules, Holy, Spirit, Counselor, Listen, Heart, Light, On, Ignore, Love
Helper

Fun Time #12

H	E	B	G	D	Z	M	R	C	B	S	U	H	T	T
O	T	C	O	N	O	U	X	P	P	J	P	U	N	N
L	J	D	P	E	I	T	X	I	E	Y	S	E	G	P
N	Q	V	V	R	S	N	D	I	S	X	I			
L	A	M	S	I	L	I	W	H	T	U	B	L	Q	
J	O	R	I	G	T	C	U	L	A	S	G	E	N	E
G	L	V	P	R	K	H	O	P	E	F	U	L	I	Q
M	G	X	E	O	A	F	X	J	T	F	G	I	T	E
C	J	P	T	F	Z	C	B	Q	Q	T	T	E	R	G
R	E	K	R	O	W	Y	L	A	E	H	J	V	J	N
V	Q	H	X	T	L	G	G	E	F	S	R	E	O	E
X	E	A	R	E	O	N	G	I	T	E	R	F	A	T
X	M	D	J	Y	A	R	P	R	B	L	B	N	A	S
E	C	D	N	X	J	W	U	Z	W	M	W	G	T	I
B	U	L	O	Y	A	L	U	P	G	V	Q	D	U	L

Answer Key

Fun Time #13	Fun Time #14
David–Jesse Joseph–Jacob Jacob–Isaac Seth–Adam Ishmael–Abraham Abraham–Terah Solomon–David Noah– Lamech	(word search grid)

Fun Time #16	Fun Time #17
Across 1. Parents 4. God 5. Confess 7. Salvation 8. Sinners 9. Sin Down 2. Rules 3. Young 5. Christian 6. Believe	But the counselor, the Holy Spirit whom the Father will send in my name will teach you all things and will remind you of everything I have said to you. (John 14:26 NIV)

Fun Time #18	Fun Time #19
Treat others as you want them to treat you. (Matt. 7:12)	It, sit, spit, spot, top, pot, rot, hot, hop, its, slit, pit, rip, trip, sip, lot, lit, this, ship, slot

Fun Time #23	Fun Time #24
Let your hope make you glad. Be patient in time of trouble and never stop praying. (Rom. 12:12)	Across 1. Food 4. No 5. Repent 7. Pray 8. Yes 9. Jesus Down 2. Disobedience 3. Bible 6. Thank

Remember to checkout my website for frequently asked questions by children, group discussion questions and resources to help you be intentional in your children's spiritual development.

Other titles by Kathy Kirk: *Let's Talk About Salvation*

Upcoming titles in My Child's Heart Series:

What Goes In Must Come Out
My Friends and Siblings Are Driving Me Crazy
I Don't Like Being Told What to Do

How to Reach Us

For more information, visit our "My Child's Heart" website! Log on to www.MyChildsHeart.org to discover new resources, activities, Bible Q&A and ideas to help you and your children develop a life that is pleasing to God.

Pleasant Word

To order additional copies of this title call:
1-877-421-READ (7323)
or please visit our Web site at
www.pleasantwordbooks.com

If you enjoyed this quality custom-published book,
drop by our Web site for more books and information.

www.winepressgroup.com
"Your partner in custom publishing."